THE
FAMILIAR
AND
THE
UNFAMILIAR
IN
TWENTIETH-
CENTURY
ARCHITECTURE

THE
FAMILIAR
AND
THE
UNFAMILIAR
IN
TWENTIETH-
CENTURY
ARCHITECTURE

JEAN LA MARCHE

UNIVERSITY OF ILLINOIS PRESS
URBANA AND CHICAGO

∞ This book is printed on acid-free paper.

Library of Congress
Cataloging-in-Publication Data

La Marche, Jean.
The familiar and the unfamiliar in
twentieth-century architecture /
Jean La Marche.
p.   cm.
Includes bibliographical references
and index.
ISBN 0-252-02785-X (alk. paper)
1. Architecture, Modern—20th century.
I. Title.
NA680.L32   2003
724'.6—dc21   2002004452

To all those who have dedicated
themselves to an understanding
of architecture and the human
experience

On the one hand, it [*"just mainte-nant"* ("just now")] does not hap-pen to a constituted *us,* to a human subjectivity whose essence would be arrested and would *then* find itself affected by the history of this thing called architecture. We appear to ourselves only through an expe-rience of spacing which is already marked by architecture. What hap-pens through architecture both con-structs and instructs this *us.*

—Derrida, "Point de Folie—
    Maintenant L'architecture"

CONTENTS

FIGURES

ACKNOWLEDGMENTS

There are several people who have provided extraordinary assistance in the completion of this book. Among those, I am especially grateful to Deborah Koshinsky for her help in editing and Scott Nunemaker for his help in tracking down images. Others who were of great help at the conclusion of this project include Carol Ann Fabian, Ken Schmitz, and Kevin White. Their assistance was of great consequence and I will always appreciate their generosity and dedication. For help in all areas concerned with this book, I thank Beth Tauke, whose support and criticism have been invaluable.

THE
FAMILIAR
AND
THE
UNFAMILIAR
IN
TWENTIETH-
CENTURY
ARCHITECTURE

INTRODUCTION

Perhaps the most enduring image of the architectural subject—the person that architects imagine experiencing their architecture—is the drawing of the "Vitruvian man" by Leonardo da Vinci (fig. 1). This image has been widely published in books used in architecture classes in the United States and elsewhere, imprinting on the minds of thousands of young students its iconic status and its message concerning the relationship between the human body and abstract geometry as demonstrated in the basic forms of the square and the circle.[1] There are some who have criticized the use of this drawing as a standard, however, because it limits the ways in which others have imagined the subject. Some critics have raised questions about this image as a representation of the male domination of the architectural world.[2] Some have expressed concern about the healthy, muscular, and ideal condition of the figure in relation

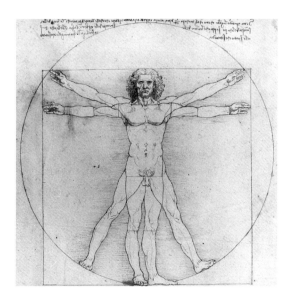

Figure 1. Drawing, "Vitruvian man," Leonardo da Vinci, c. 1485–90. (Courtesy Soprintendenza per il Patrimonio storico artistico e demoetno-antropologico di Venezia)

to the various populations that architecture serves. Given the various ways in which humans are imagined in relation to architecture, challenges also have been made about the use of the body as the best representation of human experience. Although the senses have been extolled by empiricists for centuries as the source of truth, they also have been criticized by rationalists for their susceptibility to distortion and illusion. Still others have questioned the proposed integral relationship between the human body and the perfect geometric forms of the circle and the square, including the possibility of the integration of body and mind that the "Vitruvian man" suggests. Questions have been raised, as well, about the promise of wholeness and unity from the perspective that such promises are delusional, if one assumes that the subject is fragmented, multiple, and dynamic: the artifice of unity excludes these and other possible subjects (fig. 2).

In this book I will examine some of these issues as I explore the ideas of the familiar and the unfamiliar in twentieth-century architecture. I will do so by examining the work, both written and built, of four seminal architects or firms in the twentieth century. I will refer to the subjects that emerge from this analysis as imagined because I will uncover them from the theorized descriptions of those people (*not* the specific clients) whom the architects discuss in their written texts. Supplemented with relevant theories and criticism presented in twentieth-century thought in general and in architectural theory in particular, this understanding of the subject will become the basis for an examination of the architecture that the authors produced.

I would frame the discussion by invoking the subjects of two of the primary voices in twentieth-century architecture: Sigfried Giedion and Bernard Tschumi. Perhaps the most important voice of European modernism in the

Figure 2. Ivan Chermayeff, Polaroid self-portrait, undated. (Courtesy of the artist)

second quarter of the twentieth century, Giedion made widely influential contributions to this topic, and his argument about the subject had the potential for shaping an entire generation's concept of it. He stated that "[we] have behind us a period in which thinking and feeling were separated. This schism produced individuals whose inner development was uneven, who lacked inner equilibrium: split personalities."[3] Giedion argued that this imbalance continued in the modern subject and that architecture should be used to overcome it.

> At the moment when there is a schism, the inner kernal of personality is split by a difference of level between the methods of thinking and those of feeling. The result is the symbol of our period: the maladjusted man. . . . It is he who must be integrated—integrated in his inner nature, without being brutalized, so that his emotional and intellectual outlets will no longer be divorced by an insuperable difference of level. To bring this fact into consciousness and to try to overcome it is closely connected with the outstanding task of this period: to humanize—that is, to reabsorb emotionally—what has been created by the spirit . . . [and] to create again the whole man, unfractured in his methods of thinking and feeling.[4]

Giedion insisted on the ideal of an integrated subject over what K. Michael Hays has termed "the disintegrating determinants of matter."[5] For Giedion, this served as the primary objective of architecture in the modern era.

At the end of the twentieth century, Bernard Tschumi argued that the pleasure of architecture was based on the movement between the intellectual and the physical.[6] Pleasure resulted from the movement between the material experience of the physical and the non-material experiences of the abstract, in a sense, between the body and the mind. Architecture set in motion "the operations of seduction" through "the dialectic between the sensible and the intellectual, the concrete and the abstract."[7] Such movement and its pleasures depended on the split for their operation.

While Tschumi and Giedion agreed about the structure of the subject (that it was split) and even about one of two aspects of their respective subjects (they both defined the intellectual as an important mode of human experience), they were less in agreement about the second mode: Giedion's "feeling" is not the same as Tschumi's "physical." Although not mutually exclusive, balance and movement as Giedion's and Tschumi's respective objectives are quite different. For Giedion, an imbalance was unacceptable and architecture was to be used to help overcome it. For Tschumi, a certain imbalance was necessary for the possibilities of movement and pleasure, and architecture was to sustain it. In fact, pleasures depended on the "undoing of synthesis," as Derrida described it.[8]

In order to identify the ways in which architecture could pursue these pleasures, Tschumi argued that it was necessary to "defamiliarize" its subjects:

> In recent years, small pockets of resistance [to a postmodern turn to signs] began to form as architects in various parts of the world—England, Austria, the United States, Japan (for the most part, in advanced postindustrial cultures)—started to take advantage of this condition of fragmentation and superficiality and to turn it against itself. If the prevalent ideology was one of familiarity—familiarity with known images, derived from 1920s modernism or eighteenth-century classicism—maybe one's role was to defamiliarize. If the new, mediated world echoed and reinforced our dismantled reality, maybe, just maybe, one should take advantage of such dismantling, celebrate fragmentation by celebrating the culture of differences, by accelerating and intensifying the loss of certainty, of center, of history.[9]

Tschumi considered the strategy of defamiliarization so important that it was one of the "Six Concepts" he advocated as relevant to late twentieth-century culture. He cited Walter Benjamin's argument from the classic essay "The Work of Art in the Age of Mechanical Reproduction" to support his position as stated in the second concept, "The Mediated 'Metropolitan' Shock."

> When Benjamin discussed the reproducibility of images, he pointed out that the loss of their exchange value, their "aura," made them interchangeable, and that in an age of pure information the only thing that counted was the "shock"—the shock of images, their surprise factor. This shock factor was what allowed an image to stand out: moreover, it was also characteristic of our contemporary condition and of the dangers of life in the modern metropolis. These dangers resulted in constant anxiety about finding oneself in a world in which everything was insignificant and gratuitous. The experience

of such anxiety was an experience of defamiliarization, of *Un-zu-hause-sein,* of *Unheimlichkeit,* of the uncanny.[10]

Tschumi is correct in claiming that defamiliarization was a widely shared intention in architecture at the end of the twentieth century (although not specifically referred to as such). He aids us in recognizing other practices similar to that of defamiliarization when he compares it to the uncanny, a topic of considerable interest in some theoretical circles. This interest was evident, for example, in Anthony Vidler's collection of essays published under the title *The Architectural Uncanny: Essays in the Modern Unhomely* in 1994. Other theorists were interested in related experiences, such as the sublime, the abject, and the grotesque.[11] Deconstructivist architecture was the most frequently cited expression of these experiences.[12]

Defamiliarization was of interest not only in the late twentieth century but throughout the century. It was especially apparent in early modernist architecture, work that has been characterized as focused on the "shock of the new."[13] The new was considered a means of cultural transformation. Defamiliarization—although that is not the term that was used at the beginning of the century—arose automatically when architects carefully attended to certain convictions about "economy of means" and produced an architecture focused on the honest expression of structure, materials, and functions and not on the styles of the past. The strategy of defamiliarization was important if architecture was to be relevant and appropriate to the age. Because the age was new, the architecture had to be new as well: the old architecture would simply obstruct the possibilities of a new architecture in full correspondence to the modern era and the sensibilities that it would inevitably produce. Whenever architects take this position, they assume that architecture is to be used to introduce the new, to embody it in the spaces and the experiences made possible by new materials. They passionately believe in the power of architecture to shape our values, ideas, aesthetic preferences, and even the ways we think and imagine. Modernists generally believed that past architecture was unable to support new sensibilities and, in fact, that it deterred the development of sensibilities appropriate to the new, modern era. It was important, therefore, to present the characteristics of the new age in architecture, even if they were shocking to people.

At the end of the twentieth century, Tschumi repeated this conviction and the strategies associated with modernism by claiming that "shock is still all we have left to communicate in a time of generalized information."[14] He stated that architecture's purpose lay in "accelerating and intensifying the loss of certainty, of center, of history."[15] Derrida concurred, stating that "I would say that we should not be afraid, because as you know modern or so-called postmodern architecture has been charged with being barbarian, ignoring or destroying the beautiful norms with which we are familiar. We should not be scared by some barbarity."[16]

Tschumi was not alone in finding the familiar suspect. As Mark Wigley has pointed out, "Derrida has taught us how to question the familiar—indeed, following Heidegger, to be suspicious particularly of the familiarity of the ingrained intellectual practices that organize both so-called high-cultural institutions . . . and the so-called practices of everyday life."[17]

At the core of the critique of the familiar lay the suspicion that it reinforced and satisfied conventional, popular interests in the comfort and security provided by permanence, order, and authority. It affirmed the status quo. Critics assumed that the familiar carries with it an "outworn essence of truth,"[18] that is, that our assumptions about truth are related to the familiar.

None of the authors whose works I examine below actually used the term "defamiliarization." Nonetheless, those who practiced in the early part of the century—Frank Lloyd Wright and Le Corbusier—adamantly rejected the familiar styles of the past, in favor of what they argued was "new." They believed that the familiar presented certain assumptions about truths that were no longer historically relevant or appropriate. The familiar also forestalled certain liberations and obstructed the possibilities of the free play of life, as Nietzsche suggested, by allowing only certain kinds of behavior and certain ways of seeing and thinking; as Derrida put it, "some political authority is embodied in architecture."[19]

As the twentieth century progressed and the "new" became associated with modernism, modern architecture evoked a sense of alienation, and questions arose concerning its relevance to contemporary subjects. In the early 1970s, architects turned once again to the familiar as the basis for their work. They believed that the familiar activated memory and association and thus guaranteed relevance and meaning. Architects of this persuasion drew upon architectural "types" and vernacular buildings because of their common accessibility. In addition, they turned to contextualism as a means of blending new buildings with local contexts instead of contrasting with them, as modernists had done.

The interest in designing architecture in such a way as to avoid the alienation in modernism was a fundamental motivation of the reemergence of typological and contextualist theory in the 1960s.[20] Two of the architects or firms whose work I will examine, Aldo Rossi and Venturi Scott Brown and Associates (VSBA), were primary contributors to this widely shared return to the familiar. Tied to the revival in Italy, Rossi adhered to the tenets of the early, formal version of typology and contextualism, which was more European. Venturi and Scott Brown were engaged in the early formal approach and later in the American, cultural version, referred to as "cultural contextualism,"[21] that developed at Cornell University.[22] The differences in attitudes and philosophical propensities between Rossi and VSBA became most apparent in their opposing sources and scales of contextual referents. Rossi's method of analyzing the city, for example, was based on preoccupations with the Gestalt concept of figure-ground relationships in the urban plan.[23] He introduced this method in his seminal work, *The Architecture of the City,* which I will examine more closely below.

Although Rossi's contextualist practice was patterned after the traditional materialistic attitude which dictated that "the design must fit with, respond to, mediate its surroundings, perhaps completing a pattern implicit in the street layout or introducing a new one,"[24] the American version expanded the concept to include the social context. Based on an approach to urban design that had its antecedent in the "'vest pocket utopias' of the Renaissance . . . which followed their own interior line of development, but with subtle contextual accommodations at the interface with the existing urban fabric,"[25] cultural contextualism showed a "deference towards the existing situation and pragmatic manipulations of the periphery."[26] The work of VSBA, as evidenced in the firm's addition to the Allen Memorial Art Museum at Oberlin College, included aspects of both the European and the American approaches.[27]

Certain architects assumed that the familiar activated memory and association. It is not surprising that those who relied on types made no serious attempt to transform human experience; in fact, it is precisely the already familiar visual, bodily, and temporal experiences that constituted one of the great values of conventional types of buildings. By contrast, modernism's loss of continuity with the past was the result of a historical break, a rupture so significant that it made it possible—in fact, necessary—to reconfigure the experiences of the eye and the body in order to be sympathetic to the new and changing modern world.

In 1991, Tschumi posed the following question: "Is the experience of architecture something that is meant to defamiliarize—let's say, a form of 'art'—or, on the contrary, is it something that is meant to be comforting, *heimlich,* homely—something that protects?"[28] The four architects whose work I will examine will divide along the lines of the question of the familiar and the unfamiliar. I will explore their writings and their buildings to uncover some of the ways in which these ideas are employed in architectural theory and practice. This process will be useful in comparing intentions and objectives concerning the "orientation" of the subjects that architects imagine and will allow us to speculate about how the subject is theorized in architecture.

There is not necessarily a historical trajectory in architecture that leads simply from a concentration on defamiliarization in the early part of the twentieth century to one on the familiar in the latter part. The emergence of contextualist interests at the end of the twentieth century coincided with the continuation of the modernist interest in defamiliarization, as Tschumi's statements demonstrate.[29] This should make us cautious about concluding that there is a direct path from early to late twentieth-century theory and practice in relation to these issues. Additional study would reveal a pattern of the coexistence of these two propensities throughout the century.

The present study is complicated by the fact that the definitions of the terms "familiar" and "unfamiliar" are problematic. Freud had already raised one dimension of the problem in his study of the uncanny. In his conclusions to his study, he argued that the concept of the homely (*heimlich,* familiar) and that of the uncanny or strange (*unheimlich,* or the results of the process of defamiliarization) are related. In fact, he concluded that they are co-dependent: the uncanny should be understood in relation to the familiar. The one cannot exist without the other.

The study of the familiar and the unfamiliar is further complicated by the problem of identifying the characteristics of each. What is familiar to one person might be strange and disturbing to another. In addition, there are multiple interests in architecture, which has been valued for many different reasons across time and cultures. If we reflect on the various arguments put forward in the last two centuries alone, architecture has been appreciated for its evidence of sacrifice, obedience, humility, and honesty (Ruskin); utility; historicist value (Giedion, Tschumi, and many others); and as a "repository of human labor" (Rossi). According to Mikhail Bakhtin, "the object [read 'architecture'] reveals first of all precisely the socially heteroglot multiplicity of its names, definitions and value judgements. Instead of the virginal fullness and inexhaustibility of the object itself, the prose writer confronts a multitude of routes, roads and paths that have been laid down in the object by social consciousness. Along with the internal contradictions inside the object itself, the prose writer witnesses as well the unfolding of social heteroglossia surrounding the object, the Tower-of-Babel mixing of languages that goes on around any object."[30] The history of Western architectural theory is replete with evidence of this variety.

Our study is also made more difficult by the various purposes that have been assigned to architecture. Classical architecture, for example, has been regarded as "edifying" or ennobling; it was intended to help foster "better" values. Modernists believed that architecture should be used to liberate an oppressed population and to transform culture and the individuals who participate in it; it was intended to create a socially enlightened and free people. Those who advocated honesty in architecture, such as John Ruskin, assumed that such an architecture would promote the same values in people. Depending on the time and geographic location, architecture has been intended for well being, social "good" behavior, civitas, and even pleasure.

Each individual work of architecture is also the repository of many "voices" embedded and embodied in it. These include those who design it; those who physically produce (make or manufacture) it; those who want or need to use it; and those who variously facilitate or obstruct its production, delivery, or use. Architecture is also multifunctioning, a condition that depends upon the ways in which we are oriented toward it. We examine it, at different times, in terms of craft, materials, concept, function, form, or imagery. From this perspective, therefore, architecture is a collective artifact. The idea of the familiar and the strange and the appetite for each varies among cultures, communities, and individuals as it does in relation to history and mood.

The idea of the subject has become problematic as well. The term is complicated by its two primary and contradictory meanings: the active subject of individual consciousness and the passive subject with an ideologically produced consciousness. The subject is either "that which thinks, feels, perceives, intends"[31]—a subject that acts—or "that which undergoes or may undergo some action,"[32] often one of control, influence, or domination, a subject that is acted upon. The contradictory meanings of the subject as active agent and as passive recipient of action introduce a level of complexity in the study of the subject that one should bear in mind in reading the architectural texts in this book.

The clarity of the idea of the subject is diffused by the varieties of subjects that have appeared in the past and that continue to appear in the present. The proliferation of subjects that began with the increasing specialization of knowledge (each discipline explicitly or implicitly defines a subject possibility) and the fragmentation of the disciplines in the nineteenth century escalated in the twentieth. Each theory about the subject introduced more complexity and richness as well as more conflict. By the 1990s, the definition of the subject was undecidable. The characteristics and traits that were ascribed to the subject were so radically dissimilar and contradictory and so changeable that a consensus was impossible. The concept of a fixed personality or a universal human nature collapsed under the weight of the complex array of terms applied by various disciplines and individuals and the radically opposed conceptions of freedom and determination that each assumed. In addition, late twentieth-century studies eroded the longstanding convictions about who the people were for whom architecture was designed.[33] As Richard Sennett has argued, "the codes of inwardness and unity which have shaped our culture [since the Renaissance] . . . [have made] it difficult to cope with the facts of diversity."[34]

Some theorists have even announced the end of the subject per se, arguing that it is an invented concept that serves a particular ideology.[35] Recent interest in defamiliarization and familiarization coupled with a concern for nostalgia, anxiety, and the uncanny, however, demonstrate that a considerable amount of attention to the subject and its ideological service does not negate its impact on the body of knowledge developing around this topic.

Although the questions are difficult, they are also important. As Derrida wrote, "[o]n the one hand, it ['*just maintenant*' ('just now')] does not happen to a constituted *us,* to a human subjectivity whose essence would be arrested and would *then* find itself affected by the history of this thing called architecture. We appear to ourselves only through an experience of spacing which is already marked by architecture. What happens through architecture both constructs and instructs this *us.*"[36] Acting like a mirror, the space(s) of the mirror (Derrida's architecture) makes us appear to ourselves, shows us who we are. In doing so, it constructs as well as instructs us. An analysis of the imagined subject by means of the familiar and the unfamiliar and its relationship to works of architecture makes it possible to begin to understand the extent and manner of architecture's influence on us. The exploration below will help us understand some of these issues and the attendant complexities that make them important in architecture.

In the following chapters, I will examine these possibilities by focusing on the texts of a few influential architects in the twentieth century.[37] These architects were chosen not only because they designed and built some of the most important works of architecture in the century but also because they wrote extensively on the topic of twentieth-century architecture itself. Their work, therefore, strongly influenced other architects and yet went beyond the discipline's inner circles to influence people in the broader culture. Their works also shed light on the issues and strategies of defamiliarization and the familiar.

While examining the texts, I will look for evidence concerning how the architects imagined these concepts and, subsequently, what they assumed were the structures and characteristics of the subjects for whom they imagined their works. In this examination, I will explore how architectural subjects are constructed (their structure) and what modes of experience are assumed. I will attempt to use this information to understand the architects' intention toward their imagined subject and how they attempted to shape their architecture for it.

The architects whose work I will examine include Frank Lloyd Wright, Le Corbusier, Aldo Rossi, and the partnership of Robert Venturi and Denise Scott Brown. I will treat the work of the latter two as the product of one firm, Venturi Scott Brown and Associates (VSBA).[38] Each of these architects produced significant buildings in the twentieth century,[39] and each wrote influential texts that contain some of the most important theoretical propositions on architecture in that century.[40] In addition, each of these architects presented ideas explicitly or implicitly demonstrating interest in defamiliarization or the familiar, concepts that I will attempt to discover in their buildings. The texts include Wright's "The Art and Craft of the Machine," "The Sovereignty of the Individual," and "In the Cause of Architecture";[41] Le Corbusier's *Towards a New Architecture*;[42] Rossi's *The Architecture of the City*;[43] and Venturi's *Complexity and Contradiction in Architecture*.[44]

The following study will examine these publications as an introduction to architectural thinking. It will use the thematic framework of the familiar and the unfamiliar to develop an understanding of the subject that the architects imagine in their work. It will also touch on essential questions about how they imagine the nature and purposes of architecture and the role of the architect. This investigation will offer new perspectives on architecture and its criticism and will help us to articulate and frame questions concerning the politics and ethics of the discipline with these concerns in mind.

1 FRANK LLOYD WRIGHT

[O]ur country places a life-premium
upon Individuality as the highest
possible development of the
individual consistent with a
harmonious life of the whole.

—Frank Lloyd Wright,
"The Sovereignty of the Individual"

Frank Lloyd Wright's early essays were not concerned with the "familiar" except as an impediment to works that were appropriate for the modern era. Rather, his interest was in the new age that, because of "the Machine," as he termed it, was producing strange, new forms.[1] He considered these forms at times disagreeable. His greatest interest was in creating an architecture that would be "organic" in relation to the modern forces transforming the design and construction of buildings. New machines were producing new materials that led to new construction methods and spanning capabilities and, thus, new spaces. These forces exerted such influence on the present that nothing of the past, including its architecture, was appropriate for the emerging new world. Nothing familiar had the capacity to respond to modern needs; the more we examine them, he maintained, "the more we will find the utter helplessness of old forms to satisfy new conditions."[2] Convinced of the profound effects that architecture can have on people, Wright argued that the old forms would have negative effects on modern individuals. He believed that there had to be an "organic" relationship among history, form, and human sensibility.

The present historical era had two major issues that differentiated it from the past: the machine and the new democracy in America. Wright argued that the machine had begun to change the way in which architecture could be constructed and was starting to create new forms and spaces upon which a new architecture would be based. This architecture, Wright contended, had to be developed in an "organic," "natural" relationship to the new and specific historical moment and to all the material processes by means of which the new world became physically manifested.

According to Don Gifford, there were three major effects of the machine; it "1) changed systems and materials of construction; 2) changed the needs for and uses of architectural structures; and 3) profoundly altered our sense of the beautiful and the useful and their interrelation."[3] Therefore, as Wright saw it, it was impossible for "old forms to satisfy new conditions." Gifford goes further, touching on the thoroughness of the consequences for humans: "Of these three, the first two can be measured and documented. The third is elusive, difficult to measure and document. But it is this third effect that teases the mind because it suggests a profound alteration in our ways of thinking."[4] In the final chapter of this study I will touch on recent concerns about the impact of architecture on human thought, but it should be understood that most architects believe their work shapes the ways humans perceive, think, and imagine.

Like most of his contemporaries in Europe and America, Wright assumed that the modern era was sufficiently and distinctly separated from the past and so was the modern subject. Wright used the term "organic" to define the relationship between all of the subjects and objects of any one historical era. Reflecting Emerson's writings, which he read often, as well as his own Unitarian upbringing, Wright viewed everything in an age as organically related and subjects and objects as modified by the same forces. The architectures of the past were no longer relevant and, from Wright's point of view, they were detrimental to the health of the modern subject.

The depth of Wright's conviction can be discerned in his discussion of the central importance of "the Machine," which he thought would not only influence "the artist's techniques in building" but also be the means to create "a new social order."[5] The consequences of the widespread application of machines and industrial production in architecture meant the introduction of new materials (such as steel and reinforced concrete) and new construction methods. Steel and concrete could span greater distances than any other materials in the history of architecture. Longer spans meant larger spaces. These new materials also made it possible to reduce the overall mass of buildings constructed of masonry, a material that required greater mass than new materials to achieve the same structural ends. New materials reduced the thickness of walls and made it possible to use more glass, which could be manufactured in increasingly larger sheets. In turn, this made it possible to open interior rooms to each other and to the exterior as well. The boundary between formerly segregated spaces as well as between inside and outside began to disappear, and a new architecture that could embody Wright's interests in freedom became possible.

New materials and spaces also fostered new sensibilities. Like many others, Wright believed that the production of new forms in the modern age affected the preferences and perceptions of modern subjects. Not only did technological change transform the material conditions in which people lived and worked, but it also altered their aesthetic preferences. Making the same argument from an opposite point of view in the middle of the nineteenth century, John Ruskin (whose opinions Wright generally respected) objected to the use of iron in architecture in part because he considered it disturbing. He argued that he and his contemporaries had been accustomed to masonry structures, such as those made of bricks, built of materials that required greater massing than iron but that had shorter spanning capabilities. Slender iron structural supports were regarded as simply too thin by those whose visual habits and preferences had been shaped by a specific proportionate relationship between structure and space. Iron changed this relationship, and Ruskin complained about the visual and emotional disturbance this caused him. He wrote that architecture "having been, up to the beginning of the present century, practised for the most part in clay, stone, or wood, it has resulted that the sense of proportion and the laws of structure have been based, the one altogether, the other in great part, on the necessities consequent on the employment of those materials; and that the entire or principal employment of metallic framework would, therefore, be generally felt as a departure from the first principles of the art."[6] He expands on this point: "the fact is, that every idea respecting size, proportion, decoration, or construction, on which we are at present in the habit of acting or judging, depends on presupposition of such materials: and as I both feel myself unable to escape the influence of these prejudices, and believe that my readers will be equally so, it may be perhaps permitted to me to assume that true architecture does not admit iron as a constructive material."[7] Although Wright generally agreed with Ruskin, he believed Ruskin to be incorrect in his rejection of this new material. He believed that the emergence of the machine, which had not had as great an impact on Ruskin's life as on his own, had such a significant influence that it separated the past, with its attendant visual preferences, from the present. This meant that new visual preferences that were appropriate to the modern era were emerging.

Given his belief in an organic, historical era, Wright believed that the machine's effect on visual preferences was inevitable: "the machine . . . made possible a cleanly strength, an ideality and a poetic fire that the art of the world has not yet seen."[8] Modern individuals, according to Wright, were developing a sense of new spaces, new capabilities and new sensibilities that were emerging at the same historical moment as the rise of democratic interests, which he attempted to translate into new freedoms of movement and thought. Wright assumed that the responsibility of architecture was to be organically relevant to the new era and to participate in the transformation of human aesthetic preferences. A new architecture would help "adjust" or accommodate the subject to the new and unfamiliar yet liberating potential of the new world.

Architecture's responsibility was to "orient" subjects to the new principal truths, as he saw them, which included honest expression and freedom. In order for a new architecture to be created, it had to express honestly the age and support the concept of freedom, which Wright considered an integral part of the new world. Space was a new means by which the arts, especially architecture, could demonstrate correspondences with the emergent, modern world; exterior form reflected an interior spatial condition.

The interest in the causal relationship between inside and outside was evident in several ways in the late nineteenth century, many of which can be understood through the use of the concept of transparency.[9] The interest in transparency was already expressed in such works as those of Freud in psychology and psychoanalytics, as well as those in the sciences, such as Röntgen's development of the X ray. In each case, the psyche or the body becomes "transparent," making it possible to explore aspects of human beings that, until the modern era, remained difficult to address.

Transparency was also an essential condition of a democratic society. According to Philip Fisher, there are four characteristics of "an undamaged, democratic social space. . . . 1) It is atomistic or cellular and therefore identical from place to place. . . . 2) It is unbounded. . . . 3) [It] is transparent and intelligible. . . . Within uniformity all places and individuals replicate the features of one's own life. The lives of others become spontaneously intelligible to me. . . . The neighborhood is a sphere of intelligibility or transparency . . . [and] 4) [It] provides for no observers, for no oppositional positions. There are no outsiders. Everyone present is already a member, a participant, a citizen."[10] He continues:

Democratic society grounds itself in what we might call a Cartesian social space, one that is identical from point to point . . . so that one part can stand for or represent the whole. Democratic social space would, ideally, be a universal and everywhere similar medium in which rights and opportunities are identical, a space in which the right and even the ability to move from place to place is assured. . . . Along with mobility, the right to enter or to exit would equally be fundamental to a Cartesian social space. Similarity, representation, the absence of limits, openness to immigration and expatriation, internal mobility: these would seem to be essential features, and conspicuously Cartesian ones, of a continuous and democratic social space.[11]

Fisher also argued that the identity of subjects in a democratic society was "transparent to every other within society. . . . If thoughts are valid they must be 'yours as much as mine' or they 'are nothing.'"[12]

This idea holds true for every part of the whole as well as for the whole itself.[13] It defines the individual in relation to the greater society: each American would reflect in his or her behavior and beliefs identical democratic principles. Each could represent any other person, as long as he or she shared the same ideas of freedom. According to Fisher, "[d]emocratic social space has no clear logic of limitation because it begins with the modern notion of political representation. . . Representation, of course, also implies an identity from point to point so that one part can stand for or represent the whole." As he suggests, "[d]emocratic social space would, ideally, be a universal and everywhere similar medium in which rights and opportunities are identical, a space in which the right and even the ability to move from place to place is assured."[14] Fisher described the virtues of the new democratic individual espoused by Walt Whitman, one of Wright's favorite poets, from this perspective.

The most remarkable implication of his [Whitman's] aesthetics . . . [was] the transparency and cellular identity that he assumes between himself and all of his countrymen that he sees around him. . . . The great litany is designed around a syntax that repeats the formula "just as you . . . so I." . . . [F]or Whitman the politics of any aesthetics within a democratic social space requires that there exist experiences across time that not only will happen in identical ways but will be noticed—that is, arouse attention—and will even produce the same feelings within people living centuries apart. . . . Whitman . . . imagines himself to be doing only what anyone would do or see. He imagines himself to be having an inevitable, natural, and therefore timeless experience.[15]

According to Lionel Trilling, Whitman "wanted, both in his person and his art, to stand for all that was 'democratic' in American life, by which he meant whatever was free, impulsive, and accepting."[16] Whitman, like Wright, wanted to express the American temperament.[17]

At the same time, however, Wright considered it paramount to express individuality. As he noted, "our country places a life-premium upon Individuality as the highest possible development of the individual consistent with a harmonious life of the whole."[18] In fact, he claimed that the expression of individuality constituted the "new architectural problem."[19] The new architecture could express the spirit of individuality from the inside, corresponding "with the right to freely move."[20] Wright went even further. He believed that architecture should "portray" the "character" of the new and modern subject.

In order to address Wright's specific understanding of these objectives, it is important to examine one of the most important concepts—for some, the primary prescription of the modern era and one advocated by Wright's mentor, Louis Sullivan—"form ever follows function." Sullivan introduced this idea in his essay "The Tall Office Building Artistically Considered," where he claimed that "[a]ll things in nature have a shape, that is to say, a form, an outward semblance, that tells us what they are. . . . Unfailingly in nature these shapes express the inner life. . . . Yet the moment we peer beneath this surface of things . . . how startling is the silence of it, how amazing the flow of life, how absorbing the mystery."[21] He added, "[t]he pressure, we call Function: the resultant, Form,"[22] and explained more fully what he means by this in *Kindergarten Chats*.

> [I]t stands to reason that a thing looks like what it is, and, vice versa, it is what it looks like. . . . [S]peaking generally, outward appearances resemble inner purposes. For instances: the form, oak-tree, resembles and expresses the purpose or function, oak; the form, pine-tree, resembles and indicates the function, pine; the form, horse, resembles and is the logical output of the function, horse. . . . And so does the form, man, stand for the function, man; the form John Doe, means the function, John Doe. . . . And so the form, Roman architecture, means, if it means anything at all, the function Roman; the form, American architecture, will mean, if it ever succeeds in meaning anything, American life . . . and so on, and on, and on, and on—unceasingly, endlessly, constantly, eternally—through the range of the physical world—visual, microscopic, and telescopic, the world of the senses, the world of the intellect, the world of the heart, the world of the soul . . . a universe wherein all is function, all is form.[23]

Sullivan assumed that there was a clear and undisguised relationship between an interior and an exterior, making the exterior metaphorically transparent. In Sullivan's and Wright's architecture, the idea of form following function meant the expression of an internal space or room in the exterior form. Wright called this the third dimension: "A sense of the third dimension in the use of the 'box' and the 'slab'—and a sense of the room within as the thing to be expressed in arranging them are what made Unity

Temple; instead of the two-dimension-sense of the traditional block mass sculptured into architectural form from without."[24] (See figs. 3, 4.) The same is true of all of Wright's buildings at this time (figs. 5, 6).

Architecture characterized the spirit of the new democracy and the new age by expressing the interior spaces on the exterior, making the architec-

Figure 3. Frank Lloyd Wright, Unity Church (Temple), Oak Park, Illinois, 1906. (Courtesy The Frank Lloyd Wright Archives, Scottsdale, Arizona)

Figure 4. Frank Lloyd Wright, interior, Unity Church (Temple), Oak Park, Illinois, 1906. (Courtesy The Frank Lloyd Wright Archives, Scottsdale, Arizona)

Figure 5. Frank Lloyd Wright, Larkin Company Administration Building, Buffalo, New York, 1904. (Courtesy The Frank Lloyd Wright Archives, Scottsdale, Arizona)

Figure 6. Frank Lloyd Wright, interior, Larkin Company Administration Building, Buffalo, New York, 1904. (Courtesy The Frank Lloyd Wright Archives, Scottsdale, Arizona)

ture "transparent" and therefore making it possible to understand the interior on the exterior. Whether or not it was possible to literally see into the interior, its space served as the basis for the exterior form of the building.

Thoreau applied the same idea of transparency to individuals and buildings alike.

> What of architectural beauty I now see, I know has gradually grown from within outward, out of the necessities and character of the indweller, who is the only builder,—out of some unconscious truthfulness, and nobleness, without ever a thought for the appearance and whatever additional beauty of this kind is destined to be produced will be preceded by a like unconscious beauty of life. The most interesting dwellings in this country, as the painter knows, are the most unpretending, humble log huts and cottages of the poor commonly; it is the life of the inhabitants whose shells they are, and not any peculiarity in their surfaces merely, which makes them picturesque; and equally interesting will be the citizen's suburban box, when his life shall be as simple and as agreeable to the imagination, and there is as little straining after effect in the style of his dwelling.[25]

For Wright, the expression of the life of the individual and the collective democratic society was the monumental task and only legitimate basis for a new architecture. Sullivan clearly expressed the importance of this issue: "But how is a people to take its bearings unless the individual reckons with himself? And when I say the individual I mean you! I mean myself! I mean the specific, localized sense of the individual. To discuss architecture as a specific art is interesting enough in a way. But to discuss architecture as the projected life of a people is another story. That is a serious business. It removes architectural thought from a petty domain . . . and places it where it belongs, an inseparable part of the history of civilization."[26]

Wright believed that architecture should "portray" the individual and he designed his buildings as "portraits" of his clients. In "The Sovereignty of the Individual" he stated:

> America—a democratic republic—more than any nation poses this new architectural problem. In democratic spirit at least, her institutions are (professedly) conceived. This should mean that our country places a life-premium upon Individuality as the highest possible development of the individual consistent with a harmonious life of the whole . . . Believing, too, that the whole to be worthy as complete must consist of individual units, great and strong in themselves, not units yoked from outside in bondage but united by spirit from inside with the right to freely move, resist aggression or invasion, but only each in its own sphere. . . . [This] still is now the more or less conscious Ideal of every man truly "American." . . . Individuality then is a great, strong national Ideal. . . . In America each [person], then, does have this peculiar, inalienable right to live his life in his own house in his own

way. . . . So his home-environment may now face forward and portray his own character by way of his own "tastes" and preferably his ideas (if he has any).[27]

In an excellent essay entitled "Wright's Written People," Russell Ellis raises this point as an important aspect of our ability to interpret Wright's imagined subject. He quotes Wright's discussion of this and, in so doing, raises once again the question concerning the individual in a society of shared democratic values: "Shimmering, iridescent cages of steel and copper and glass in which the principle of standardization becomes exquisite in all variety. Homes? Growing from their site in native materials, no more 'deciduous' than the native rock ledges of the hills, or the fir trees rooted in the ground, all taking on the character of the individual in perpetual bewildering variety."[28]

Wright's interpretation of his clients is evident in his attempt to characterize them in abstractions of form, space, light, composition, and mood. According to Jack Quinan,

> [I]n 1903 when Frank Lloyd Wright was being considered as architect of the Larkin Administration Building in Buffalo, he made an unusual claim to his prospective clients that has gone unheeded by historians and critics ever since. . . . [One client reported to another,] "Mr. Wright says . . . [that] he studies his client and builds the house to fit him." . . . Three years later Wright wrote to another potential client, Avery Coonley, in a similar vein: "I try to make each home characteristic of its owner always and an interpretation when possible. I think all the buildings are entitled to a certain family resemblance in so far as they concern each other, but feel that I have failed if I do not fix the character of the building and the atmosphere of the environment, where it belongs, with the client."[29]

Wright then suggested a comparison of his architecture with the portraits of John Singer Sargent. He made this claim a third time in his essay "In the Cause of Architecture," in the *Architectural Record* of March 1908, including his comparison to Sargent, and then concluded that "[t]he individuality of an owner is first manifest in his choice of his architect, the individual to whom he entrusts his characterization. He sympathizes with his work; its expression suits him and this furnishes the common ground upon which client and architect may come together. Then, if the architect is what he ought to be, with his ready technique he consciously works for the client, idealizes his client's character and his client's tastes and makes him feel that the building is his as it really is to such an extent that he can truly say that he would rather have his own house than any other he has ever seen."[30]

With this in mind, Quinan sets out "to reinterpret the Darwin Martin house in the light of Martin's personality and Wright's claim that his houses were expressive of their clients."[31] His specific conclusions, although prelim-inary, are insightful. Quinan writes that success in business "enabled Dar-win Martin to attempt to satisfy the two yearnings that had haunted him since the death of his mother in 1871: to make a home for himself, and to reassemble the fragments of his scattered family."[32] Martin commissioned a complex of buildings in Buffalo that would include his own house (figs. 7, 8) and the Barton House (figs. 9, 10), a dwelling for his sister and her husband. Quinan points out that Martin's deepest personal concerns are "manifest-ed most significantly in the plan of the Martin complex. Wright's placement of the Martin and Barton houses at the opposite corners of an incomplete rectangle (the conservatory is on the third corner) provides graphic evidence of Martin's only concrete success in reuniting his family."[33] The floral hemi-cycle and the Nike statue had the potential of recalling Martin's mother, and the matrix established by the pergola and the conservatory made it possi-ble to imagine other houses for family members, such as the Barton House, located on the spine or on the orthogonals that emerged from the conser-vatory.

Another way that Wright's architecture was intended for the new world could be seen in the freedoms it offered, resulting largely from the effects of the machine and the enhanced capacities of the new materials that it pro-duced. Democratic principles could be expressed in architecture, for example,

Figure 7. Frank Lloyd Wright, Darwin D. Martin House, Buffalo, New York, 1904. (Courtesy the Buffalo and Erie County Historical Society, Buffalo, New York)

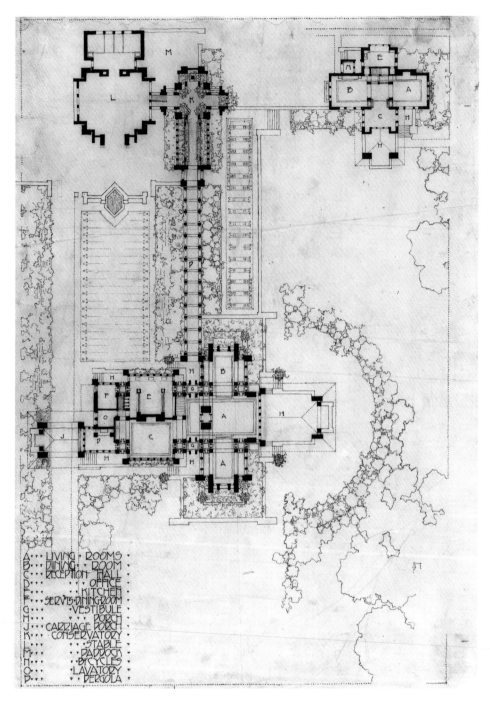

A···LIVING·ROOMS·
B···DINING·ROOM·
C···RECEPTION·HALL·
D····OFFICE·
E····KITCHEN·
F···SERVTS·DINING·ROOM·
G····VESTIBULE·
H····PORCH·
J···CARRIAGE·PORCH·
K···CONSERVATORY·
L····STABLE·
M····PADDOCK·
N····BICYCLES·
O···LAVATORY·
P···PERGOLA·

Figure 8. Frank Lloyd Wright, plan, Darwin D. Martin House Complex, Buffalo, New York, 1904. (The Drawings of Frank Lloyd Wright copyright © The Frank Lloyd Wright Foundation, Scottsdale, Arizona)

Figure 9. Frank Lloyd Wright, George Barton House, Buffalo, New York, 1903.

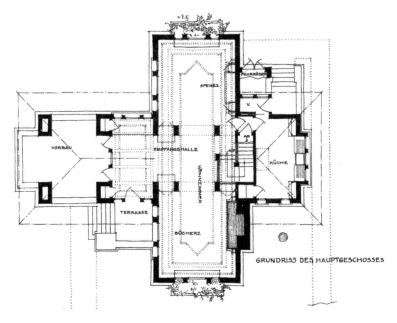

Figure 10. Frank Lloyd Wright, plan, George Barton House, Buffalo, New York, 1903.

because of the machine's ability to make architecture available to everyone in the new democratic culture. Wright writes that "[t]he machine, by its wonderful cutting, shaping, smoothing, and repetitive capacity, has made it possible to so use it without waste that the poor as well as the rich may enjoy to-day beautiful surface treatments of clean, strong forms. . . . The machine . . . has placed in artist hands the means of idealizing the true nature of wood harmoniously with man's spiritual and material needs, without waste, within reach of all."[34] Some of these freedoms were evident in the process of building; as he stated, "the Machine [was] the tool which frees human labor, lengthens and broadens the life of the simplest man, thereby the basis of the Democracy upon which we insist."[35]

In addition, Wright believed that the new forms produced by the machine and the economies of production that its simple forms expressed would be "understood" by all: "surely this would be a practical means to make their dutiful obedience give us something we can all understand, and that will be as normal to the best of this machine age as a ray of light to the healthy eye; a real help in adjusting the Man to a true sense of his importance as a factor in society."[36] The "healthy eye" belonged to the individual who was attuned correctly to the new and modern forces helping to shape the architecture for the new world.

The most important means by which Wright was able to imagine an architecture designed to advance his ideas of freedom had to do with new structural materials which, as we indicated earlier, made larger spaces possible and, simultaneously, reduced the need for walls. This made it possible to open up spaces to one another on the interior, and to open the interior to the exterior as well. The reduction of the opacity of walls and the elimination of barriers created at least two opportunities for the new architecture to present experiences of freedom. These were the freedom to move and the freedom to see. This created a liberating architecture because, in contrast to traditional architecture that used walls to separate functions and create small rooms or cells, Wright's buildings allowed people to move freely through space. According to Christian Norberg-Schulz, "[t]he wall thus is no longer used to enclose space, but it is there 'to bring the outside world into the house and let the inside of the house go outside.' . . . Continuity of space and form thus became the distinguishing principle of his organic architecture. . . . Wright also fully realized the importance of glass as 'a resource to liberate the new sense of space.' . . . [The Prairie] House therefore fulfills Wright's idea of a dwelling which both protects and liberates."[37]

Discussions of Wright's work often suggest he gave more attention to the eye, most explicitly when he describes the world as being brought to us through apertures, as though we are sedentary viewers.[38] Yet, the ability to both see and move through space was increased and facilitated in the new architecture by Wright's attention to the experience of movement.[39] The design of movement in Wright's architecture enhanced the subject's experience of freedom. This was most evident in the design of the path from the exterior to the hearth, that is, from the outside to the inside center of the house. Richard Etlin traces the evolution of Wright's thought about this movement, demonstrating the rapid if uneven progression from "the frontal and axial alignment at the Winslow House," which contained a conventional "front door," to the placement of entrances that were difficult to find.[40] Upon opening the door of the Winslow House, "the visitor enters into a reception hall where several steps lead up to a niche that contains the fireplace set within a broad brick wall, the 'integral fireplace'" (figs. 11–13).[41] The front door is easy to find and the movement to the hearth is direct. Later projects, such as the Hickox and Bradley houses, situate the entry to the side through the porte cochère and the path to the hearth becomes more adventurous (figs. 14–17). While the Frank Thomas and Arthur Heurtley houses celebrate the entrance once again, it is not aligned with the chimney, and movement sequences continue to evolve (figs. 18–22). Finally, in the Robie House, the entrance is removed entirely from view. In addition, Wright is able to make the hearth stand out on the inside and the outside, demonstrating its status as the "center" or heart of the house (figs. 23–25).[42] By the time of the Robie House, therefore, the entrance disappears and the hearth emerges in significance, exerting both centrifugal and centripetal effects on its subjects and interior spaces.[43]

Among the most important and successful architectural innovations that made freedom evident in physical and visual terms was the use of beams and curtains to separate interior spaces (Martin House) and the arrangement of rows of "French" doors on exterior walls (Martin and Robie houses) to increase the flow of space between inside and outside. If the curtains were drawn back, the interior beams suggested that walls had been removed, creating a spatial matrix of absent walls. Whenever subjects moved through the framework defined by these elements, they passed through the traces of former barriers, now phenomenally "transparent," and emerged on the other side without any resistance whatsoever, except for that created by the mental drag of our familiar, unconscious expectations of conventional separations between rooms or functions. This manifested a new architectural experience of freedom. These visual and physical experiences were organized to orient us to the hearth. Public, internal views and circulation in the more mature Prairie Houses moved toward and orbited around this "center," reminding everyone, inside and out, of its presence. The fire at the center of the hearth, at the center of the home, anchored the home to the earth and organized the landscape around it.

The other issues that Wright considered important in his work directly related to the human experience of "presence" and scale. In the Wasmuth portfolio, for example, he argued that the work that he presented in the collection could not "be intelligently studied apart from environment."[44] He insisted that his work had to be experienced in order to be understood. Drawings and photographs could not do justice to his architecture or replace the direct experience of it: "Photographs do not adequately present these subjects. A building has a presence, as has a person, that defies the photographer, and

Figure 11. Frank Lloyd Wright, W. H. Winslow House, River Forest, Illinois, 1893. (Courtesy the Frank Lloyd Wright Archives, Scottsdale, Arizona)

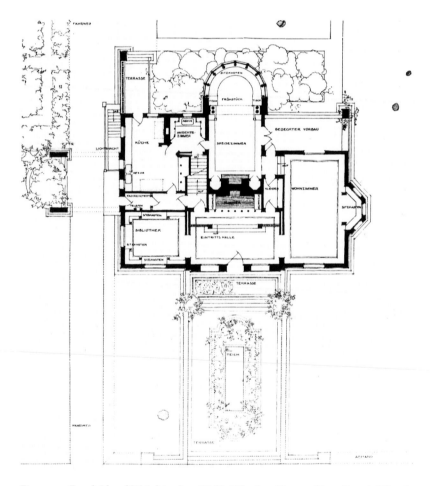

Figure 12. Frank Lloyd Wright, plan, W. H. Winslow House, River Forest, Illinois, 1893. (The Drawings of Frank Lloyd Wright copyright © The Frank Lloyd Wright Foundation, Scottsdale, Arizona)

Figure 13. Frank Lloyd
Wright, interior, W. H.
Winslow House, River
Forest, Illinois, 1893.
(Courtesy the Frank
Lloyd Wright Archives,
Scottsdale, Arizona)

Figure 14. Frank Lloyd Wright, Warren Hickox House, Kankakee, Illinois, 1900.
(Courtesy the Frank Lloyd Wright Archives, Scottsdale, Arizona)

Figure 15. Frank Lloyd
Wright, ground-floor
plan, Warren Hickox
House, Kankakee, Illi-
nois, 1900. (The Draw-
ings of Frank Lloyd
Wright copyright ©
The Frank Lloyd
Wright Foundation,
Scottsdale, Arizona)

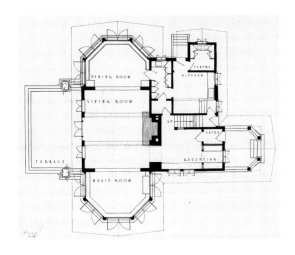

Figure 16. Frank Lloyd Wright, B. Harley Bradley House, Kankakee, Illinois, 1900. (Courtesy Ave Maria Fine Art Gallery, Ann Arbor, Michigan)

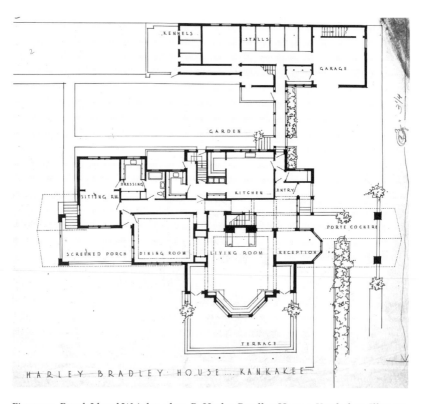

Figure 17. Frank Lloyd Wright, plan, B. Harley Bradley House, Kankakee, Illinois, 1900. (The Drawings of Frank Lloyd Wright copyright © The Frank Lloyd Wright Foundation, Scottsdale, Arizona)

Figure 18. Frank Lloyd Wright, Frank Thomas House, Oak Park, Illinois, 1901.
(Courtesy the Frank Lloyd Wright Archives, Scottsdale, Arizona)

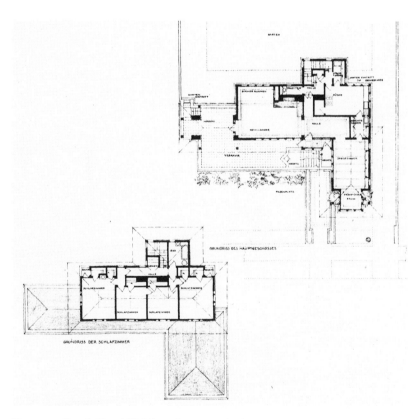

Figure 19. Frank Lloyd Wright, plans, Frank Thomas House, Oak Park, Illinois,
1901. (The Drawings of Frank Lloyd Wright copyright © The Frank Lloyd Wright
Foundation, Scottsdale, Arizona)

Figure 20. Frank Lloyd Wright, Arthur Heurtley House, Oak Park, Illinois, 1902. (Courtesy Ave Maria Fine Art Gallery, Ann Arbor, Michigan)

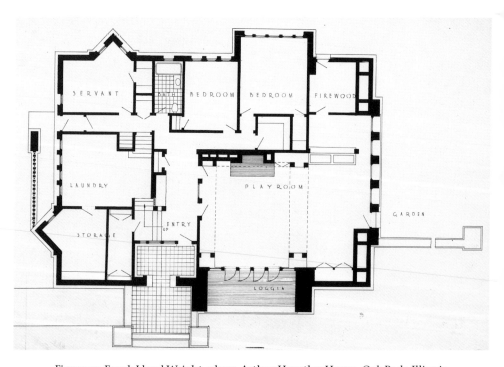

Figure 21. Frank Lloyd Wright, plans, Arthur Heurtley House, Oak Park, Illinois, 1902. (The Drawings of Frank Lloyd Wright copyright © The Frank Lloyd Wright Foundation, Scottsdale, Arizona)

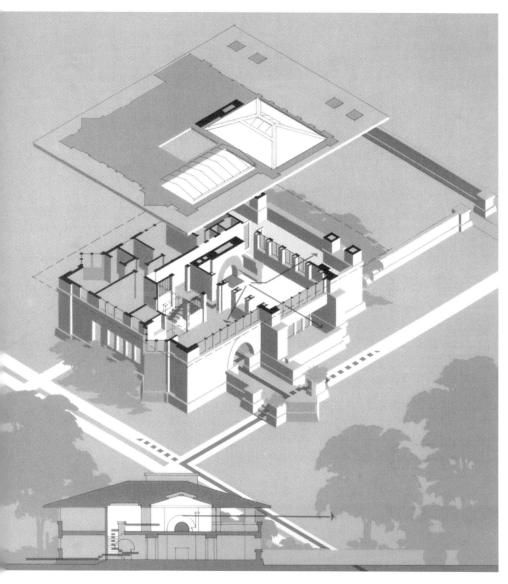

Figure 22. William Hook, diagrammatic drawing of movement, Arthur Heurtley House, Oak Park, Illinois, 1902. (From Grant Hildebrand, *The Wright Space: Pattern and Meaning in Frank Lloyd Wright's Houses* [Seattle: University of Washington Press, 1991], 37, reprinted courtesy William Hook and with permission of the University of Washington Press)

Figure 23. Frank Lloyd Wright, Frederick C. Robie House, Chicago, Illinois, 1906. (Courtesy the Frank Lloyd Wright Archives, Scottsdale, Arizona)

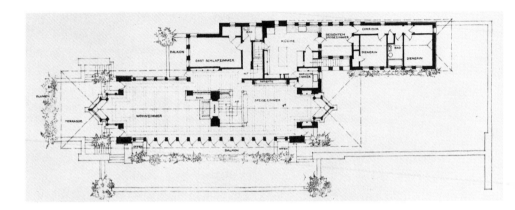

Figure 24. Frank Lloyd Wright, plan, Frederick C. Robie House, Chicago, Illinois, 1906. (The Drawings of Frank Lloyd Wright copyright © The Frank Lloyd Wright Foundation, Scottsdale, Arizona)

Figure 25. Frank Lloyd Wright, interior, Frederick C. Robie House, Chicago, Illinois, 1906. (Photograph by Henry Fuerman, courtesy the Rare Book and Special Materials Collection, Media Union Library, University of Michigan)

the color so necessary to the complete expression of the form is necessarily lacking."[45] Direct experience and "presence" were conveyed in part by the natural materials Wright used, which evoked the warmth or coldness associated with them. In addition, the idea of presence included the scale of human beings. In discussing the Coonley House at Riverside (fig. 26), as an example, Wright declared that "the style of the Coonley home is due to this simple use of materials with a sense of the human figure in scale."[46] He repeated this concern in other texts as well: "But, from one basic idea all form or formal elements of design are in each case derived and held firmly together in human-scale and appropriate character."[47]

In the end, under the influence of the romantic American poets and philosophers in the nineteenth-century, Wright developed a theory about an architecture that reflected the individuality of Americans living in a democratic society and that supported the freedoms he thought were necessary if the democracy was to survive and improve. For Wright, this meant an architecture that would support the new democratic society and its subjects by responding to the new historical era. In Wright's hands, architecture was redefined to reflect both the individual and the collective and to provide new freedoms.

In their shared democratic values as well as their individuality, Wright's clients were portrayed in their architecture and would be able to find themselves reflected in it. They would be given open spaces and transparencies that made possible new experiences of freedom in vision and movement. An

Figure 26. Frank Lloyd Wright, Avery Coonley House, Riverside, Illinois, 1907–8. (Courtesy the Frank Lloyd Wright Archives, Scottsdale, Arizona)

architecture that could succeed in affecting subjects in this way would be sympathetic to the new modern sensibilities and would support the new democracy. It would be appropriate and relevant, exhibiting conditions that would be, in a sense, "familiar" to those harboring the new democratic sensibilities.

Wright's work and his philosophy of architecture differed significantly from those of Le Corbusier, the architect we will consider in chapter 2, although the two pursued very similar agendas. Wright often criticized Le Corbusier's architecture as well as his self-propagandizing through publications, something for which Wright was also later criticized. Nonetheless, like Wright, Le Corbusier believed that the new forms produced in the modern era were strange and disturbing, and he dedicated himself and his work to making the strange familiar.

2 LE CORBUSIER

Disturbed by the reactions which play upon him from every quarter, the man of today is conscious, on the one hand, of a new world which is forming itself regularly, logically and clearly, which produces in a straightforward way things which are useful and usable, and on the other hand he finds himself, to his surprise, living in an old and hostile environment.

—Le Corbusier, *Towards a New Architecture*

Le Corbusier employed the term "familiar" only twice in *Towards a New Architecture*, which attests somewhat to his interest in what he regarded as the disturbing yet appealing quality of the new forms being produced in the modern era. These were forms determined not by conventional stylistic preferences but by logic, clarity, and economy. The infrequency with which he used related words such as "everyday," "ordinary," "normal," "conventional," and "customary"—which he employed almost exclusively as disparaging terms—corroborates his disregard for the familiar. "Architecture is stifled by custom," he wrote.[1] He proved especially critical of conventional housing, calling it "an old and hostile environment."[2] Modern subjects lived with the "stifling accumulation of age-long detritus."[3]

The old world was anathema to the modern spirit. Le Corbusier supported the logic and clarity of new forms, even though they were unfamiliar, strange, and disturbing: "The form and appearance [of modern machines] are in no way preconceived, *they are a result;* they may have a strange look at first sight. Ader made a 'Bat,' but it did not fly; Wright and Farman set themselves the problem of sustaining solid bodies in air, the result was jarring and disconcerting, but it flew."[4]

If successful, the new forms would be accepted and become part of the common, everyday stock of forms that every culture produced. According to Frederick Etchells, who first translated Le Corbusier's *Vers une architecture* as *Towards a New Architecture,* disagreeable forms can be assimilated, which is demonstrable through the study of history: "It is inevitable that the engineer, preoccupied with function and aiming at an immediate response to new demands, should produce new and strange forms, often startling at first, bizarre and disagreeable. Some of these forms . . . become friendly to us and take their place as part of our general equipment."[5] This is possible because human beings are eminently adaptable. Etchells writes, "The truth is that man has an uncanny faculty of adapting himself to new conditions. He learns to admit and even, in a sneaking sort of way, to *like* new and strange forms. The new form is at first repugnant, but if it has any real vitality and justification it becomes a friend. The merely fantastic soon dies."[6]

In architecture, according to Le Corbusier, new materials and new construction methods had generated new and unfamiliar forms and spaces. Like Wright, Le Corbusier believed that these were transforming modern visual interests. Recent historical progress—new materials and new production methods (and their resulting forms)—had changed the world, in fact, "more than the last six centuries have done."[7] These changes signaled a "deep chasm between our own epoch and earlier periods . . . not only . . . the preceding period at the beginning of the nineteenth century, but . . . the history of civilizations in general."[8] It was a historical gap that called for new needs, a new state of mind, and a new spirit.

Le Corbusier thought that these changes were most evident in the places in which people worked. The logic, simplicity, and clarity of the factory, workshop, or office provided visual interest and comfort to those imbued with the new spirit. But the new working environment was in direct opposition to the domestic environment.[9]

In the workshop, in the technical departments, in the learned Societies, in the banks and in the great stores, on newspapers and reviews, there are the engineers, the heads of departments, legal representatives, secretaries, editors, accountants who work out minutely, in accordance with their duty, the formidable things which occupy our attention: there are the men who design our bridges, ships and airplanes, who create our motors and turbines, who direct the workshops and yards, who are engaged in the distribution of capital and in accountancy, who do the purchasing of goods in the colonies or from the factory, who put forth so many articles in the Press on the modern production of so much that is noble and horrible, who record as on a chart the high-temperature curve of a humanity in labour, in perpetual labour, at a crisis—sometimes in delirium. All human material passes through their hands. In the end their observation must lead them to some conclusion. These people have their eyes fixed on the . . . modern age . . . spread before them, sparkling and radiant . . . on the far side of the barrier! In their own homes . . . they find their uncleanly old snail-shell.[10]

Le Corbusier, like Giedion, assumed that the disturbance caused by this historical split produced a demoralizing effect on the new modern state of mind. Both viewed the disjunction between these two conditions to be so serious, and the consequences of new forms on modern subjects so important, that their lack of resolution threatened the stability of society. This problem could be "ameliorated" by means of an architecture that brought people face to face with the new forms and the new logic. One of the more important contributions that Le Corbusier made to architecture was the creation of a dialectical architecture by means of which he could set up a dialectic between the past and the present, embodied in their respective spatial conditions. He did so in the houses he designed. The resolution of this modern disturbance simply required an adaptation: individuals would become familiar and comfortable with the forms and sensibilities produced by the needs of the new world.[11] Should these issues not be addressed, Le Corbusier prophesied social revolution: "If this fact [mass production] be set against the past, then you have revolution, both in the method employed and in the large scale on which it has been carried out. . . . Our minds have consciously or unconsciously apprehended these events and new needs have arisen, consciously or unconsciously. The machinery of Society, profoundly out of gear, oscillates between an amelioration, of historical importance, and a catastrophe. . . . It is a question of building which is at the root of the social unrest of today: architecture or revolution."[12] The architect's task and architecture's purpose is to make these new and strange forms familiar and to create or support the new spirit that was capable of seeing and enjoying them.

In order to pursue this new architecture, Le Corbusier made certain assumptions about the nature of the modern subject. First of all, his subject needed to have certain "universal" requirements fulfilled. These included basic physical, psychosomatic, and cultural needs.[13] All humans, he argued, shared these requirements.[14] However, he also assumed a split in the subject between the intellectual (the higher satisfactions of the "mind") and the "sensorial,"[15] and he privileged the "higher" satisfactions of the mind—mathematics, geometry, and proportion (those qualities and characteristics of value to those with "calculating minds")—over the satisfactions of the senses—the "elementary," "lesser," "cruder," or "animal" sensations:[16] "Every human manifestation involves a certain quantum of interest and particularly so in the aesthetic domain; this interest may be of an order dealing with the senses or of an intellectual order. Decoration is of a sensorial and elementary order, as is colour, and is suited to simple races, peasants and savages. Harmony and proportion incite the intellectual faculties and arrest the man of culture."[17] Although he did not deny the demands of sensation,[18] he preferred "the higher satisfactions (mathematics)" as appropriate for a modern culture.[19] He wrote, "The mouldings of the Parthenon are infallible and implacable. In severity they go far beyond our practice, or man's normal capabilities. Here, the purest witness to the physiology of sensation, and to the mathematical speculation attached to it, is fixed and determined: we are riveted by our senses; we are ravished in our minds; we touch the axis of harmony."[20] (See fig. 27.)

The new spirit responded to these new visual interests. If properly attuned to the modern era, this spirit was excited and satisfied by geometry as

Figure 27. Detail, Parthenon, Athens. (From Le Corbusier, *Vers une architecture* [Paris: G. Crès, 1924], 180)

well as other "calculated" aspects of architecture—proportion, scale, functional rationality, and the spatial, temporal, and formal changes that new technologies made possible. In recognizing these characteristics, "the eye transmits to the brain co-ordinated sensations and the mind derives from these satisfactions of a high order."[21] Le Corbusier called this new visual interest "the desire of our eyes": "architecture . . . SHOULD USE THOSE ELEMENTS WHICH ARE CAPABLE OF AFFECTING OUR SENSES, AND OF REWARDING *THE DESIRE OF OUR EYES,* and should dispose them in such a way THAT THE SIGHT OF THEM AFFECTS US IMMEDIATELY by their delicacy or their brutality, their riot or their serenity, their indifference or their interest; these elements are plastic elements, forms which our eyes see clearly and which our mind can measure" (italics added).[22]

Those modern individuals who were imbued with the new spirit would experience aesthetic pleasure at the sight of something created by logical and economical design. This pleasure, in turn, would transform into a desire for these experiences and, thus, Le Corbusier's "desire of our eyes." He considered mathematics an absolute and essential basis for all matter in the universe and thus the basis of architecture.[23] Whoever recognized this order would "resonate" with aesthetic pleasure. It was, therefore, incumbent upon architects that they develop a "mathematical genius, . . . [a] capacity for achieving order and unity by measurement and for organizing, in accordance with evident laws, all those things which excite and satisfy our visual senses to the fullest degree."[24] It was possible to work toward these ends, according to Le Corbusier, because the mind could "measure" the order of mathematics by means of human scale. Height, reach, foot, and thumb, for example, could be used to help determine the sizes and proportions of architectural elements and the relationships between them.[25] In describing the construction of a primitive temple, Le Corbusier claimed that the builder "takes as his measure what is easiest and most constant, the tool that he is least likely to lose: his pace, his foot, his elbow, his finger. In order to construct well . . . [h]e has imposed order by means of measurement. In order to get his measurement he has taken his pace, his foot, his elbow or his finger. By imposing the order of his foot or his arm, he has created a unit which regulates the whole work; and this work is on his own scale, to his own proportion, comfortable for him, *to his measure.* It is on the human *scale.* It is in harmony with him."[26] Le Corbusier believed that the use of the builder's body in the building of a work of architecture was evident in the work and could be experienced by others.

This image of the human being played an important role in Le Corbusier's anthropocentric perspective, which, according to Françoise Choay, he inherited from ancient Greece: "'One must always try to find the human scale,' says Le Corbusier . . . 'an architecture must be walked through, traversed'; it is made to be seen by our human eye placed at 63 inches from the ground. . . . [T]he height of a man, the reach of his arm, his foot, his thumb, and so on, will serve to calculate the size of doors, window, sunbreaks or pillars. . . . [M]odern man, who feels himself a stranger in the monuments or dwellings of 19th and 20th century architecture, [will] find in the buildings of Le Corbusier a wonderful feeling of security, of familiarity, a sort of happiness involving all his movements."[27]

Le Corbusier's classical leanings are also evident in his creation of the Modulor, a mathematical system of proportions based on the human figure that he used to design and refine his architecture (fig. 28).[28] The similarities between the "Vitruvian man" (see fig. 1) and the Modulor are revealing (fig. 29). Thus, Le Corbusier is adamant about the modern historical period as being new while also expressing an interest in a timeless, classical understanding of architecture.

This dialectic between the past and the present is also evident in his conceptualization of two human bodies: one is based on measure (the Modulor) and, although he would subordinate experiences of the senses to those of the

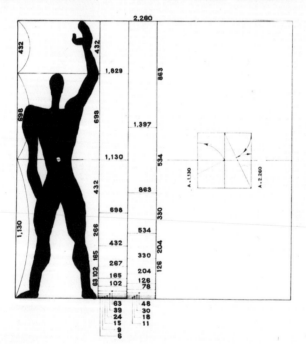

Figure 28. Le Corbusier, drawing, "The Modulor." (© 2002 Artists Rights Society [ARS], New York/ADAGP, Paris/FLC)

intellect, the other is based on sensation (the living, active body that moves through space). These were the two prevalent concepts of the body in late nineteenth-century aesthetic theory—the classical, humanist body as form or figure and the more sensible body, a dynamic, tactile, and kinesthetic body. The sensible body was very much a part of the modern era. It was characterized by a material presence and, as such, represented a relatively new realm of human experience that could be examined for its capacity to construct relevant modern experiences. New aesthetic experiences could be based on movement and such experiences were assumed to be collective, unlike former aesthetic theories that depended on aristocratic taste cultures. These new experiences, therefore, were considered liberating.

Taking the measure of a work of architecture also meant that the work had to be fully experienced, an idea that is best represented by Le Corbusier's idea of the architectural "promenade."[29] He considered the promenade es-

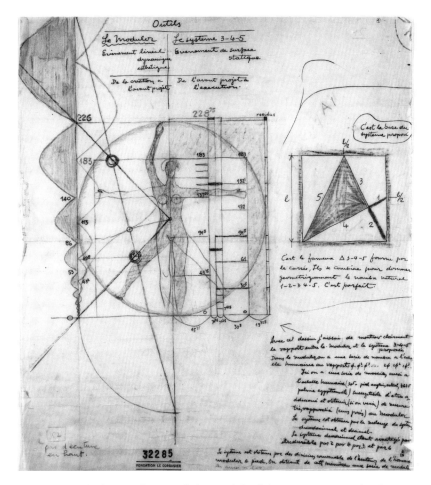

Figure 29. Le Corbusier, drawing, "The Modulor." (© 2002 Artists Rights Society [ARS], New York/ADAGP, Paris/FLC)

sential, even claiming that "[a]rchitecture can be classified as dead or living by the degree to which the rule of *sequential movement* has been ignored or, instead, brilliantly observed."[30] In 1923, with the publication of *Towards a New Architecture,* he had already made clear his commitment to the promenade. In the chapter on the illusion of plans, for example, he argued that the true axis in architecture was "a mental organization that groups a sequence of spaces into a coherent composition related to a visitor's movement."[31] In commenting about the Villa Savoye at Poissy (1929–31) he stated that "Arab architecture gives us a precious lesson. It is appreciated by walking on foot; it is by walking, by moving, that one sees the order of the architecture developing. It is a principle contrary to that of baroque architecture, which is conceived on paper, around a fixed theoretical point. I prefer the lesson of Arab architecture. In this house it's a question of a real architectural promenade, offering constantly changing views, unexpected, sometimes astonishing."[32] Beatriz Colomina points out the cinematic character of this experience:

> The point of view of modern architecture is never fixed, as in baroque architecture, or as in the model of vision of the camera obscura, but always in motion, as in film or in the city. Crowds, shoppers in a department store, railroad travelers, and the inhabitants of Le Corbusier's houses have in common with movie viewers that they cannot fix (arrest) the image. Like the movie viewer that Benjamin describes ("no sooner has his eye grasped a scene than it is already changed"), they inhabit a space that is neither inside nor outside, public nor private (in the traditional understanding of these terms). It is a space that is not made of walls but of images. Images as walls. Or as Le Corbusier puts it, "walls of light." That is, the walls that define the space are no longer solid walls punctuated by small windows but have been dematerialized, thinned down with new building technologies and replaced by extended windows, lines of glass whose views now define the space. The walls that are not transparent now float in the space of the house rather than produce it. . . . And if, as Rasmussen points out, "the walls give the impression of being made out of paper," the big window is a paper wall with a picture on it, a picture wall, a (movie) screen.[33]

Understanding Le Corbusier's architecture meant recognizing the dialectic between the past and the present that he went to such great lengths to present in his work. This became possible by the reductions of both histories to monumental forms and surfaces, reductions that often meant the loss of texture and material references.[34] Such reductions made the historical split more "graphically" visible—a strategy that made it possible to set "this fact [the present] against the past"—and, perhaps, made it less disturbing and eventually more familiar. This is the new architecture that Le Corbusier created to prevent social revolution.

Le Corbusier's propensity for dialectics is evident most clearly in his 1920s villas and maisons, in which the past was represented by abstractions of classical space (which he had studied on his journeys to the Mediterranean) and the present was acknowledged by abstractions of logical and economical constructions like machines (which he chose to represent the modern era).[35] He profusely illustrated and enlarged upon both in his texts. The characteristics of the past that Le Corbusier repeated in his work were symmetry, rhythm, and proportion. The structural bays serve as the clearest demonstration of classical spatial rhythms (along one side in bays of 2, 1, 2, 1, and 2 and along the other in bays of 0.5, 1.5, 1.5, 1.5, and 0.5) articulated by the piloti, the modern version of the column (fig. 30). The present was represented by the abstracted forms of machines arranged pragmatically and not governed by the symmetries and centering tendencies of the classical grid. Forms of mechanical sensibility were evident throughout Le Corbusier's architecture. This can be found most explicitly in such examples as the

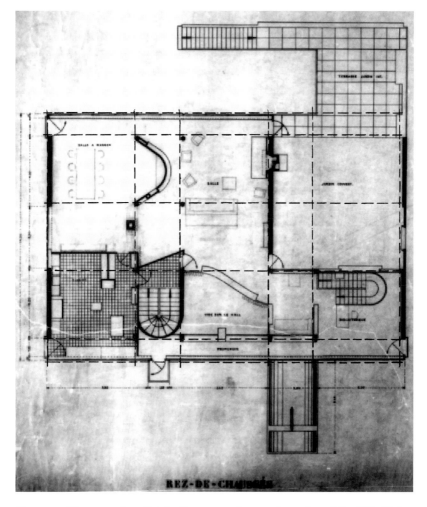

Figure 30. Diagram of spatial rhythms superimposed on plan of the Villa Stein, Garches, 1926–27. (Overlay by author, plan © 2002 Artists Rights Society [ARS], New York/ADAGP, Paris/FLC)

entry room on the ground level of the Maison Cook (fig. 31), which recalls the Farman Goliath airplane (fig. 32)—illustrated more often than any other machine in *Vers une architecture*—and the roof of the Villa Stein (fig. 33), which, like the roof of the Villa Savoye, has the feel of a ship. The juxtaposition of these two abstractions constituted an important historical framework for Le Corbusier's architecture and writings. This is perhaps clearest on certain pages of *Vers une architecture,* which carries an illustration of the Parthenon above one of the 1921 Delage Grand-Sport automobile (fig. 34).

The dialectic was activated by the promenade. Movement along it was designed to present glimpses of abstracted machine forms framed in a classically proportioned spatial matrix. It allowed the viewer to gain a sense of

Figure 31. Le Corbusier, Maison Cook, Paris, 1926. (© 2002 Artists Rights Society [ARS], New York/ADAGP, Paris/FLC)

Figure 32. Farman Goliath airplane. (From Le Corbusier, *Vers une architecture* [Paris: G. Crès, 1924], 95)

Figure 33. Le Corbusier, roof, Villa Stein, Garches, 1926–27. (© 2002 Artists Rights Society [ARS], New York/ADAGP, Paris/FLC)

Figure 34. Parthenon and a 1921 Delage Grand-Sport. (From Le Corbusier, *Vers une architecture* [Paris: G. Crès, 1924], 107)

the architecture—its geometry, proportions, and spatial rhythms as well as the logic, economy, and practicality of the functional accommodations to modern life, including the expression of construction practices as evidenced in the minimum thickness of walls (fig. 35).[36]

In the 1920s, the promenade was most clearly evident in such architectural elements as the ramp in the Villa Savoye (fig. 36). As the ramp ascends, it penetrates the horizontal plate of each floor and provides the principal means of movement from the entry on the first floor to the "picture window," the last picturesque moment on the roof and the conclusion of the promenade (figs. 37, 38). Le Corbusier's more complex and "topographic" experiences, as Colin Rowe calls them, were those in the Maison La Roche (fig. 39) and the Villa Stein at Garches (figs. 40, 41).[37]

In each of these buildings, the promenade moves through a virtual grid of pilotis arranged in classical spatial rhythms, which provides centering (the central bay in the grid is bracketed by the others and therefore is stressed). As Etlin points out,

> Le Corbusier's technique of using rows of columns to convey the sense of parallel spatial planes has been well-known in the literature of modern archi-

Figure 35. Le Corbusier, Maison La Roche, Paris, 1923. (Photo by the author)

tecture since Colin Rowe and Robert Sluztky published their essay in 1963 that defined this "phenomenal" or conceptual transparency. The term refers to a conceptual as opposed to literal transparency whereby the viewer connects the columns to form a spatial plane that passes through any intervening objects. Within the frontally gridded space created by the arrangement of columns, Le Corbusier places his walls, some straight, others curved, some defining edges, others making sculptural shapes.[38]

Fully experiencing a work of architecture required an interest in geometry as well.[39] Once again Le Corbusier turns to the builder: "But in deciding the form of the enclosure, the form of the hut, the situation of the altar and

Figure 36. Le Corbusier, Villa Savoye at Poissy, 1929–31. (© 2002 Artists Rights Society [ARS], New York/ADAGP, Paris/FLC)

Figure 37. Le Corbusier, interior ramp and spiral stairs, Villa Savoye at Poissy, 1929–31. (© 2002 Artists Rights Society [ARS], New York/ADAGP, Paris/FLC)

Figure 38. Le Corbusier, patio and ramp, Villa Savoye at Poissy, 1929–31. (© 2002 Artists Rights Society [ARS], New York/ADAGP, Paris/FLC)

Figure 39. Le Corbusier, interior, Maison La Roche, Paris, 1923. (© 2002 Artists Rights Society [ARS], New York/ADAGP, Paris/FLC)

Figure 40. Le Corbusier, Villa Stein, Garches, 1926–27. (© 2002 Artists Rights Society [ARS], New York/ADAGP, Paris/FLC)

Figure 41. Le Corbusier, interior, Villa Stein, Garches, 1926–27. (© 2002 Artists Rights Society [ARS], New York/ADAGP, Paris/FLC)

its accessories, he [the builder] has had by instinct recourse to right angles—axes, the square, the circle. For he could not create anything otherwise which would give him the feeling that he was creating. For all these things—axes, circles, right angles—are geometrical truths, and give results that our eye can measure and recognize. . . . Geometry is the language of man."[40]

Le Corbusier assumed that the interest in geometry was universal, an interest shared by modern and classical subjects alike. In describing a fragment of the Parthenon (fig. 42), for example, he called attention to its formal qualities and the impression that it made on him: "All this plastic machinery is realized in marble with the rigour that we have learned to apply in the machine. The impression is of naked polished steel."[41] Thus, modern subjects and those of Periclean Greece shared a similar sense of form, a similar "desire of our eyes" and a similar aesthetic preference: "If we are brought up short by the Parthenon, it is because a chord inside us is struck when we see it; the axis is touched."[42] Le Corbusier used the front-wheel brake of the Delage Grand-Sport to reinforce this point: "This precision, this cleanness in execution go [sic] further back than our re-born mechanical sense. Phidias felt in this way: the entablature of the Parthenon is a witness."[43] Correspondences between the past and the present are also evident in the sources for the promenade, which were both classical and contemporary:[44] the difficult and ceremonial journey up the Acropolis to the Parthenon, which Le Corbusier had visited in his youth, and the easy and leisurely perambulations or healthy walks on the decks of ships, both of which he illustrated in *Towards a New Architecture* (figs. 43, 44).

By moving through space, the subject would be presented with the coexistence of the two histories and the dialectical possibilities between them and, thus, with the possibility of their synthesis.[45] If the modern subject could "see" these "measures" in a work of architecture, she or he could experience the mathematical correspondence between the body and the cosmos, between the subject and the universe.

Sensing the relationship between the mind and the body satisfied the modern subject's mechanical sensibility and connected this subject, through proportion and scale, to the work. The harmony between body and mind was evident in the "resonance" of aesthetic pleasure experienced in the moment in which the subject "recognized" or sensed these correlations. Le Corbusier describes this experience as one in which our "axis" is struck: "If the canoe, the musical instrument, the turbine, all results of experiment and calculation, appear to us to be 'organized' phenomena, that is to say as having in themselves a certain life, it is because they are based upon that axis. From this we get a possible definition of harmony, that is to say a moment of accord with the axis which lies in man, and so with the laws of the

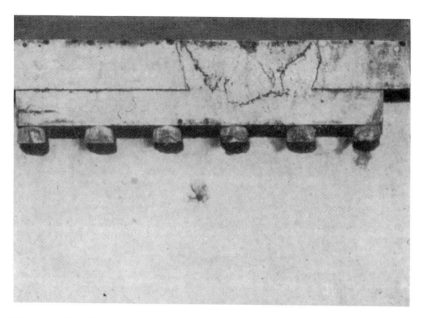

Figure 42. Detail, Parthenon, Athens. (From Le Corbusier, *Vers une architecture* [Paris: G. Crès, 1924], 178)

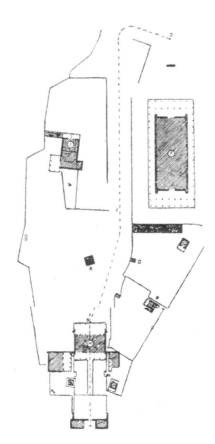

Figure 43. Plan, Acropolis, Athens; dashed line repre-sents the path of move-ment. (From Le Corbusier, *Vers une architecture* [Paris: G. Crès, 1924], 39)

Figure 44. Photograph, view of deck, *Empress of France* (Canadian Pacific). (From Le Corbusier, *Vers une architecture* [Paris: G. Crès, 1924], 78)

universe,—a return to universal law."[46] The subject's axis was the measure of harmony: "This sounding-board which vibrates in us is our criterion of harmony. This is indeed the axis on which man is organized in perfect accord with nature and probably with the universe, this axis of organization which must indeed be that on which all phenomena and all objects of nature are based; this axis leads us to assume a unity of conduct in the universe."[47] Resonance was a vibration that manifested a correspondence between the mathematics of the universe and the human body.

The correspondence between subjects and objects, between human beings and the universe, was "the desire of our eyes," a visual preference that was the responsibility of the architect to satisfy: "The Architect, by his arrangement of forms . . . affects our senses . . . and provokes plastic emotions; by the relationships which he creates he wakes profound echoes in us, he gives us the measure of an order which we feel to be in accordance with that of our world, he determines the various movements of our heart and of our understanding; it is then that we experience the sense of beauty."[48]

Yet, the superposition of these two historical abstractions—one promising a center in its rhythmic spaces and the other displacing any centralizing tendency with the pragmatically organized functional and mechanical necessities—revealed the tensions of the modern era as Le Corbusier saw them. The seemingly random, sleek, dynamic, and unfamiliar forms of the present contrasted with the centering, rhythmic assurances of the spatial matrix of the past.

Similar contradictions are apparent in Le Corbusier's imagined subject as well. Although he intended his work for a "universal" subject, this subject was required to have a certain urbane outlook and a high intellectual capacity or mental disposition. Le Corbusier establishes this dichotomy by overtly laying claim to a universal subject while simultaneously constructing an architecture that was often considered esoteric, intended only for those with eyes that could see properly. This is corroborated in his text when, ultimately, he declared his preferences for certain subjects: "Beauty governs all; she is of purely human creation; she is the overplus necessary only to men of the highest type."[49] Le Corbusier privileged the intellectual over the brute sensations and, in so doing, assigned these propensities to different populations, as when he stated that the "magnificent flowering of industry in our epoch has created a special class of intellectuals so numerous that it constitutes the really active stratum of society."[50] Each member of this new class would have a "calculating mind" and, thus, the ability to appreciate the new architecture he proposed.[51] He or she would be able to recognize it, to see it, as he claimed. At the same time, he argued that others had "eyes which do not see." Significantly, a specific visual interest separated those who had eyes to see from those who did not: those with eyes to see could do so only because they had a mechanical sensibility and an interest in evaluating the world that was appropriate to the zeitgeist, as he interpreted it.[52]

The contradictions we find in Le Corbusier's intentions are also evident in his work. Observers have described his architecture as hermetic and cryptically inaccessible. Most have viewed it as cold, austere, severe, Cartesian, logical, and, as Françoise Choay held, brutal, aggressive, and uncompromising.[53] Kenneth Frampton described it as having a "sepulchral disquiet."[54] Such disquietude, according to some critics, emanated from Le Corbusier's own "struggle, of his constant battles with the world . . . generalized beyond his own personal experience to become the major theme of his life."[55] He was an intractable figure. A man of many names, known as Charles Edouard Jeanneret until 1917, when he adopted the name Le Corbusier by which history now records his life and works, he also assumed several aliases for the papers he published in *L'Esprit nouveau*. According to Charles Jencks, the "multiple proper names mirror his complexity and elusive character."[56] He inherited his ethics from the enlightened philosophers of the eighteenth century and his social intentions from the nineteenth-century utopians who followed.[57] A rationalist with an unshakable interest in technology,[58] he was also a prophet and a mystic; his mission was moral, millennialistic, and messianic.[59] Over time he managed to be positivistic, progressive, and reactionary.[60]

According to Jencks, Le Corbusier's personal struggles culminated in a tragic view of the human condition.[61]

Aldo Rossi, the architect who is the subject of chapter 3, also exhibited certain tragic characteristics. While his architecture was intended to be familiar, it was criticized more often than not as surreal. Thus, in some ways, the effect of Rossi's architecture was the reverse of Le Corbusier's: it made the familiar strange.

3 ALDO ROSSI

In the exaggerated silence of an
urban summer, I grasped the deformation, not only of ourselves, but of
objects and things as well.

—Aldo Rossi, *A Scientific
Autobiography*

The idea of the familiar in Aldo
Rossi's work has two dimensions
that are in apparent conflict. On
the one hand, Rossi focused on the
analysis of types in architecture
because they represented collective
intentions. The types he discov-
ered through his analyses made it
possible for him to design buildings and urban formations that
were familiar to people. He wrote,
"Anyone who remembers European cities after the bombings of the
last war retains an image of disem-
boweled houses where, amid the
rubble, fragments of familiar places
remained standing, with their col-
ors of faded wallpaper, laundry
hanging suspended in the air, bark-
ing dogs—the untidy intimacy of

places. And always we could see the house of our childhood, strangely aged, present in the flux of the city."[1]

On the other hand, in the application of types in the design process, Rossi based his selections on the associations that he made with other places and objects that he found compatible. This was the basis of his later arguments for an analogical process, a process in which an array of impressions and memories, as well as objects and places, could be associated with each other to provide the basis for the design, production, and experience of architecture: "I have always had a strong interest in objects, instruments, apparatus, tools. Without intending to I used to linger for hours in the large kitchen at S., on Lake Como, drawing the coffeepots, the pans, the bottles. I particularly loved the strange shapes of the coffeepots enameled blue, green, red; they were miniatures of the fantastic architectures that I would encounter later."[2]

Personal associations abound in Rossi's *A Scientific Autobiography:*

> I read Bishop Palladio's *Historia Lausiaca* and *The Life of St. Anthony,* and I was impressed by the monks' cities, the convents scattered across the desert, and farther out, the hermits' caves. Thousands of men lived in desert monasteries as in secret cities spread out over a sun-parched region. . . . I saw something similar in Puglia, near Lucera: it was a huge, practically inaccessible crater in which caves were dug out along the vertical walls, forming a forbidding amphitheater, burned by the rays of the sun yet at the same time cold. This was the place of anchorites, brigands, prostitutes, and perdidos, and it still produces this strange impression. I saw an ancient city that was an alternative to the history of civilization; it was a city that seemed to have no history: it consisted of its people's lives, rather than the consumption of their bodies and minds. But here too there were ruins, created by nature yet always constructed out of those living relationships that exist even in solitude— ruins not unlike those of Federico di Svevia's nearby castle, or of the plan of the Arabian city, or ruins which became confounded with each other, mingling regulating lines, profiles, human bodies, architectural materials.[3]

The issue of the familiar in Rossi's work, therefore, raises certain questions about the concepts and the processes he employed and, as discussed below, the dimension of autobiography that permeates his work.

Rossi focused his analysis of architecture on the most common and most often repeated buildings and urban formations. He assumed that the repetition of certain types reflected a collective memory or will. Such collective artifacts were modified by local conditions, such as techniques of construction, materials, site, and style: "Type is thus a constant. . . . [I]t reacts dialectically with technique, function, and style, as well as with both the collective character and the individual moment of the architectural artifact. It is clear, for example, that the central plan is a fixed and constant type in religious architecture; but even so, each time a central plan is chosen, dialectical themes are put into play with the architecture of the church, with its functions, with its constructional technique, and with the collective that participates in the life of that church."[4] Types manifested "the forces that are at play in a permanent and universal way in all urban artifacts."[5] They were "essential" signs of life,[6] and, as such, they represented forms of life repeated across time and cultures. Rossi referred to them as "constant," "stable," and "timeless."[7]

The Roman amphitheater, an architectural type constructed in various locations in Europe, Asia, and Africa, stands as one of Rossi's most compelling examples. He illustrated this type several times, including examples in Arles and Nîmes in France, and in Florence, Lucca, and Rome (figs. 45–49). This building type was transformed over time in different ways in diverse locations to serve various and dynamically changing social, economic, and cultural needs. In Florence, for example, housing was eventually built into the remains of the amphitheater, and markets in the amphitheaters in Nîmes and Lucca. According to Rossi, the transformations that these types have undergone record the life and history of the community.

Understanding Rossi's design intentions helps us to comprehend his imagined subjects because he made similar assumptions about subjects and objects alike; each contained an essential, collective condition that could be individualized through local and specific histories. He has made this relationship very explicit and, in so doing, raises the question of autobiography, once again, as we saw in the earlier discussion of Frank Lloyd Wright: "Thus

Figure 45. Bird's-eye view, Roman amphitheater, Arles, late first century. (Photo reprinted by permission of Librarie Plon, Paris)

Figure 46. Plan, Roman amphitheater, Florence, late first or early second century. (Courtesy of Civica Raccòlta delle Stampe Achille Bertarelli, Milan)

Figure 47. Plan, Roman amphitheater, Nîmes, late first or early second century. (Courtesy of Civica Raccòlta delle Stampe Achille Bertarelli, Milan)

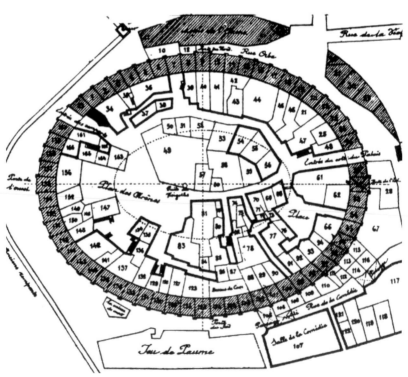

Figure 48. Bird's-eye view, houses on site of Roman amphitheater, Lucca. (Courtesy of Aldo Rossi/Studio di Architettura)

I believe that a project may be a conclusion to a chain of associations, or else may actually be forgotten and left to other people or situations. This kind of forgetting is also associated with a loss of our own identity."[8]

The relationship between subjects and objects is evident in Rossi's language in relation to both. He employed similar terms and concepts for each and assumed that they both underwent similar processes of deformation. Citing Walter Benjamin's comment that "'I am deformed by connections with everything that surrounds me here,'"[9] Rossi paraphrased this for his own purposes: "In the exaggerated silence of an urban summer, I grasped the deformation, not only of ourselves, but of objects and things as well."[10]

These correspondences are important in understanding Rossi's early work, and an examination of his own personal struggle makes this clear. Of the author-architects examined in the present book, he is the most autobio-

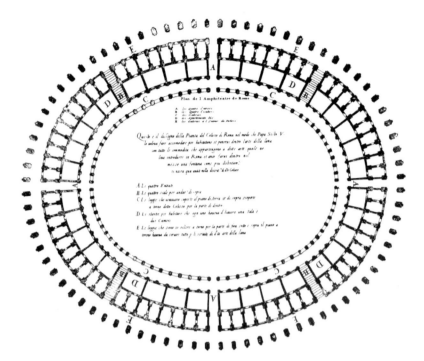

Figure 49. Plan, Colosseum, Rome. (Courtesy of Aldo Rossi/Studio di Architettura)

graphical, at least in his writings, an issue that we will examine more closely in the conclusions to this study. A brief review, however, will be helpful in understanding his work and his struggle with the question of the familiar.

We can begin to understand some of the complexity of this issue by observing Rossi's aspiration to be objective in his work, to be what he called "scientific." In order to achieve this objectivity properly, Rossi felt compelled to eradicate what he considered his "bourgeois childhood." He assumed that this dimension of his own subjectivity profoundly deformed his otherwise collective nature and, therefore, he felt compelled to erase it. Erasure would uncover the "constant," "stable," "timeless," and collective subject inside him.[11] Just as Rossi assumed he was able to uncover types in architecture by erasing the "contingencies" that deformed them, so he assumed that he could "uncover" his own collective subjectivity by erasing the "bourgeois" part of himself. The characteristics that Rossi sought in types—permanence, universality, essentiality, constancy, stability, and timelessness—matched the characteristics that he sought in himself. He "loved the rigors of science,"[12] and he found himself compelled by that abiding interest to erase those aspects that distorted the objective and scientific view to which he aspired: "Thus I have learned how to look at cities with an archaeological and surgical eye. I have disliked modernist aesthetics like any other formal revival, and as I have said, my early experience of Soviet architecture helped me to sweep away every petit-bourgeois inheritance of modern architecture."[13] Petit-bourgeois sentiments counteracted his interest in a "scientific," universal point of view and had to be eliminated.

Rossi believed the collective subject was essential and universally shared, a belief that is evident in his claim to have a view of the world that was similar to that of any other scientific or objective person. He thought, for example, that he could see his little "cabins" at Elba "like any other observer, since they are not transfixed in a single summer" (fig. 50).[14] He assumed he had the capacity to see in the same way as anyone else because of his ability to eliminate his own private, autobiographical aspects when he contemplated objects. By this means, he uncovered what he thought was his own collective subjectivity, one that he assumed was shared by everyone.

Yet some critics have criticized these assumptions by pointing to his

Figure 50. Aldo Rossi, drawing, *Le cabine dell'Elba, 1975.* (Courtesy of Aldo Rossi/ Studio di Architettura)

analogical process and the associations that he used in his designs as personal. Demonstrating his "analogical process" of associations, for example, he claimed that the little cabins at Elba "simultaneously become a wardrobe, dressing room, house, theater, small cemetery."[15] These are not necessarily the associations that we should expect others to have. For Peter Eisenman, Rossi's work was very personal and hermetic. Eisenman claimed that Rossi's work, as well as his thinking, was inaccessible to others. For this reason, he called Rossi an "autonomous researcher."[16]

This sense of inaccessibility can be seen in Rossi's early projects, which were composed of simple forms usually based on primary geometric volumes such as cubes, cylinders, and extruded triangles. Critics referred to this work as "purist."[17] Rossi's 1965 monument to the partisans of World War II for City Hall Square in Segrate, Italy, demonstrates this tendency most clearly (figs. 51–54).

A similar reductiveness imbues his middle work, between the years 1969 and 1973.[18] For example, the additions he made to the De Amicis School in Broni, Italy (1969–70), repeated some of the geometric forms of the Segrate monument (figs. 55–56). The Elementary School at Fagnano Olona, Italy (1972–76), exhibits the same, although now at a different scale (figs. 57–60). In this particular project, Rossi introduced a new size or scale of typological elements, including the cylinder, the cone, and the steps, now primary typological elements of the "architecture of the city." The housing complex of Gallaratese 2, built in Milan, Italy (1969–73), was perhaps Rossi's most

Figure 51. Aldo Rossi, plan drawing, Monument to the Partisans of World War II, City Hall Square, Segrate, Italy, 1965. (Courtesy of Aldo Rossi/Studio di Architettura)

Figure 52. Aldo Rossi, perspective drawing, Monument to the Partisans of World War II, City Hall Square, Segrate, Italy, 1965. (Courtesy of Aldo Rossi/Studio di Architettura))

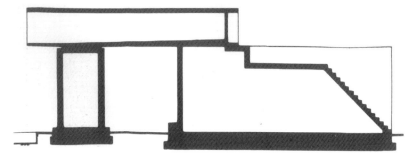

Figure 53. Aldo Rossi, section, Monument to the Partisans of World War II, City Hall Square, Segrate, Italy, 1965. (Courtesy of Aldo Rossi/Studio di Architettura)

Figure 54. Aldo Rossi, Monument to the Partisans of World War II, City Hall Square, Segrate, Italy, 1965. (Courtesy of Aldo Rossi/Studio di Architettura)

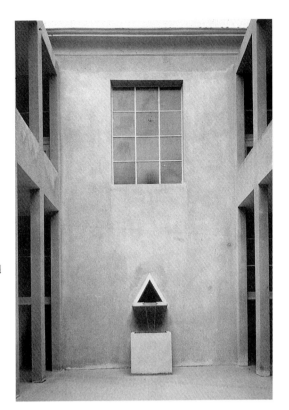

Figure 55. Aldo Rossi, interior, restoration and addition, De Amicis School, Broni, Italy, 1969–70. (Courtesy of Aldo Rossi/Studio di Architettura)

Figure 56. Aldo Rossi, restoration and addition, De Amicis School, Broni, Italy, 1969–70. (Courtesy of Aldo Rossi/Studio di Architettura)

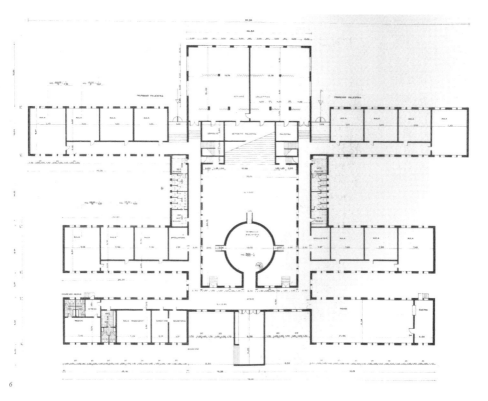

Figure 57. Aldo Rossi, plan, Elementary School, Fagnano Olona, Italy, 1972–76. (Courtesy of Aldo Rossi/Studio di Architettura)

Figure 58. Aldo Rossi, courtyard, Elementary School, Fagnano Olona, Italy, 1972–76. (© Barbara Burg / Oliver Schuh; courtesy of Aldo Rossi/Studio di Architettura)

Figure 59. Aldo Rossi,
stairs in courtyard, Ele-
mentary School, Fagna-
no Olona, Italy, 1972–76.
(© Barbara Burg / Oliver
Schuh; courtesy of Aldo
Rossi/Studio di Architet-
tura)

Figure 60. Aldo Rossi, view from interior, Elementary School, Fagnano Olona,
Italy, 1972–76. (© Barbara Burg / Oliver Schuh; courtesy of Aldo Rossi/Studio di
Architettura)

publicized work of this period (figs. 61–63). Based on one of the most widespread housing types in Lombardy—open-air single-loaded corridor housing—its design used *ballatoi*, or corridors, on the upper floors and an open-air colonnade on the ground floor.

The work of his middle years moved toward a focus on other contextual concerns: construction materials and techniques, climate, and the history of the area began to be expressed in his work and to soften the early geometric severity. The Pavilion at Borgo Ticino, Italy (1973; figs. 64, 65), designed

Figure 61. Aldo Rossi, Gallaratese 2, Milan, Italy, 1969–73. (Courtesy of Aldo Rossi/Studio di Architettura)

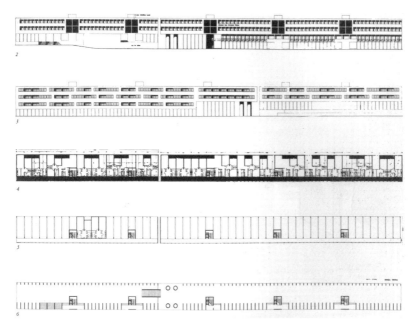

Figure 62. Aldo Rossi, plan and elevation drawings, Gallaratese 2, Milan, Italy, 1969–73. (Courtesy of Aldo Rossi/Studio di Architettura)

Figure 63. Aldo Rossi,
view down the portico,
Gallaratese 2, Milan, Italy, 1969–73. (Courtesy of
Aldo Rossi/Studio di Ar-
chitettura)

with Gianni Braghieri, repeated the volumetric forms, surfaces, and compo-
sitional strategies that one finds in Gallaratese 2. At Borgo Ticino, however,
Rossi found that these elements "express a condition of happiness; maybe
because . . . of [the] connection [between 'the plastered-brick walls . . . [and]
semicylindrical roof of sheet metal' of his Pavilion] with boathouses, with
fishermen's huts on the Ticino and Po rivers."[19] One can observe a number
of similar contextual responses in other projects.

Of all of the works that Rossi produced, the Cemetery of San Cataldo in
Modena, Italy (1971–84), was the most controversial (figs. 66–68). This work
seemed alien and surreal to many of those who critiqued it in architectural
publications;[20] it was even compared to de Chirico's paintings (fig. 69).[21] Rafael Moneo, one of Rossi's supporters, reinforced this criticism by claiming that
Rossi's work characterized "his estrangement from the real, understood as
everyday occurrence."[22] Moneo described the "emptiness" in the cemetery
as intentional and claimed its emptiness, the arrival to nothing, imparted
meaning to the approach. Emptiness became the goal of the journey. But
Rossi seemed surprised by the critical response and its scope: "I remember
how this project provoked ferocious attacks on me which I did not comprehend; attacks were even directed at my entire architectural activity."[23]

Figure 64. Aldo Rossi, Pavilion, Borgo Ticino, Italy, 1973. (Courtesy of Aldo Rossi/Studio di Architettura)

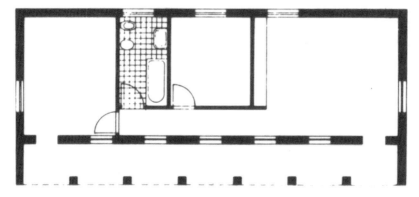

Figure 65. Aldo Rossi, plan, Pavilion, Borgo Ticino, Italy, 1973. (Courtesy of Aldo Rossi/Studio di Architettura)

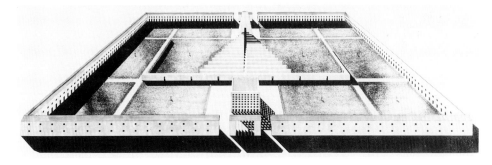

Figure 66. Aldo Rossi, with Gianni Braghieri, perspective drawing, Cemetery of San Cataldo, Modena, Italy, 1971–84. (Courtesy of Aldo Rossi/Studio di Architettura)

Figure 67. Aldo Rossi, with Gianni Braghieri, Cemetery of San Cataldo, Modena, Italy, 1971–84. (Courtesy of Aldo Rossi/Studio di Architettura)

Ultimately, many did not experience Rossi's work as he had intended. This lack of correspondence between others' experiences and Rossi's assumptions about them could be traced to the erasures necessary for the uncovering of types: his architecture presented these erasures as absence or emptiness.

Rossi already had suggested something of this sort by claiming that his architecture was "mute." Vincent Scully wrote of his work:

These forms all move to a kind of familiar affection because they seem to present us with a fundamental state of being, outside fashion, and calling

Figure 68. Aldo Rossi, with Gianni Braghieri, Cemetery of San Cataldo, Modena, Italy, 1971–84. (© Barbara Burg / Oliver Schuh; courtesy of Aldo Rossi/Studio di Architettura)

Figure 69. Giorgio de Chirico, *The Anguish of Departure,* 1913–14. (© 2002 Artists Rights Society [ARS], New York/SIAE, Rome)

into question even the concept of style, far more than the International Style ever did. They are forms which appear to be, as Rossi hoped, "without evolution." They simply are, as if they always were. Therefore they shun linguistic gestures. They are silent. Kahn, too, late in life, had called for "silence," and Rossi repeatedly states in this text that he wants his building to be "mute." He employs the German word *sprachlos* to describe them. And speechless they stand, vehicles of remembrance, touching as in some physical faculty beyond the realm of words. Speechless, we open our hearts to them, and they guard our dreams.[24]

Rossi intended his architecture to be sympathetic to collective experiences by repeating types that represented common and familiar forms of life. He employed these types to create a collective architecture designed to "invite life." As I have described this elsewhere, "the absence of traces of 'life' in the images/spaces [of Rossi's work] is what is to call forth life (the laundry on the balcony)—a dialectical strategy."[25] The "presence" of absence (erasure) is specifically that which invited the subject to live in/with the work; in so doing, architecture would acquire the traces of "life" otherwise absent, an architectural horror vacui. The erasure in objects, therefore, is not only an analytical means of uncovering types but also makes possible an architecture designed to be taken over by others.

The erasures in Rossi's early and middle work, however, remain. They culminated in an architecture so austere it contained little or no reference to time, place, or scale. The timelessness that Rossi sought haunted his work. Alan Colquhoun writes that it operated at "such a level of generality that, [the architecture is] no longer vulnerable to technological or social interference, it stands frozen in a surreal timelessness."[26] Rossi's early work is haunted by the "latency" produced by these erasures. In addition to being suffused with such undertones, this work is also haunted by several tragic possibilities, including those of a "pathological" architectural artifact, to use his terms, which cannot be absorbed by the city. Perhaps erasure tended not to invite collective traces but to prevent the take-over that Rossi intended.

The other dimension of Rossi's view that contributes to this possibility is his interest in the "strange" and the "irrational." Once more, Scully presents the case. In his postscript to the *Scientific Autobiography,* he claims that

[f]or me this book has something of the quality of a divesting. When I finished reading it I felt utterly solitary, shorn of ideologies, alone with the memory of the things I have seen. It is not a linear book; it does not begin somewhere and get somewhere. It circles. So everything is dreamlike: changing but static, revolving around fixed points of obsession. Conscious reasoning seems left behind. . . . Consequently there is no predetermined connection between things, no hierarchy. Everything is seen afresh, may be connected with other things in some new way. This is Rossi's greatest

strength; it enables his eyes to focus upon the nonrational life of objects that may be said to go on inside the brain of man but is not identical with his reason. . . . [E]verything that impedes the irrationality of perception has been gone through, cast aside.[27]

Rossi had already declared his interest in the irrational in *The Architecture of the City:* "For this reason, when I first wrote this book, its style and literary construction were of particular concern to me, as they always are, because only the perfect clarity of a rational system allows one to confront irrational questions, forces one to consider the irrational in the only way possible: through the use of reason."[28] Later, in *A Scientific Autobiography,* he would continue to manifest this interest: "rationality or the smallest degree of lucidity permits an analysis of what is certainly reality's most fascinating aspect: the inexpressible. . . . 'Strolling one evening in a forest I happened to grasp the shadow of a plant': this passage from Boullée allowed me to understand the complexity of the irrational in architecture."[29] Rossi assumed that the irrational was an important aspect of life itself: "For this reason, ever since my childhood, saints' lives and mythological stories have shown me so many things disturbing to common sense that I have forever come to appreciate a certain spiritual restlessness, something latently bizarre in the order of life."[30]

After several years, Rossi realized that his own early attempts to transform himself into an objective, collective subject had eliminated something important in his own subjectivity: "Later, the scientific bent of my research estranged me from what was most important, namely the imagination of which such relations are made."[31] Until the moment in which he recanted his early attempts to erase a part of his own subjectivity, however, Rossi's architectural subjects and objects were similar to one another. Both were conceived in binary terms and understood to be in dialectical relationships with their own local or private histories—universal type-forms and contextual or local "deformations"—as well as with each other. The marks made by contingent historical forces were those that had to be identified, separated out, and eliminated in the analysis of types: "It is only in the history of architecture that a separation between the original element and its various forms occurred. From this separation . . . derives the universally acknowledged character of permanence of those first forms."[32] He continued: "Burckhardt understood this process when he wrote, 'There, in the sanctuary, they [the artists] took their first steps toward the sublime; they learned to eliminate the contingent from form. Types came into being; ultimately, the first ideals.'"[33]

The binary constituted the basic framework of Rossi's subjects and his objects. Eisenman cited several of the binaries typical of Rossi's work: the dialectic of "permanence and growth," "remembering and forgetting," and the "giant collective house of the city and its individual, specific houses, the city's artifacts."[34] Other important binaries included the collective and the individual or bourgeois; the universal or general and the particular; and, using gestalt theory, the ground and the figure.

Every binary established the framework for dialectical transformations and, thus, for history, progress, and change. Yet, according to Rossi, change was "futile." It was "the mark of superficial people."[35] "The signs of people and objects . . . that supposedly are changeless—in fact they do change, but the change is always so terribly futile. . . . Of course . . . things change as we ourselves change. But what does this change signify? I have always considered change a characteristic of cretins, a kind of stylishness—a stylishness characterized by inconsistency."[36] Each of the subordinate terms of the binary—technique, function, or style—engages type dialectically and deforms it.

Rossi always privileged one of the two terms of the binary over the other. His search for the constant, the permanent, the type, or the collective aspects of objects and subjects—the essential and universal—contrasted sharply with what he proposed for the second term of each binary, function, technique, bourgeois sentiment—the changing and contingent factors. The first, or privileged, terms consisted of the fixed, constant, and collective. The second terms consisted of clearly deforming forces. His privileged terms shared certain similarities: types and collective subjectivities related to permanence and constancy. He ascribed subordinate terms to relativistic contingencies such as individual and bourgeois subjectivities, emotions, figure, growth, and change, all of which he deemed deformational, even futile. "When a project or a form is not utopian or abstract but evolves from the specific problems of the city, it persists and expresses these problems both through its style and form as well as through its many deformations. These deformations or alterations are of limited importance precisely because architecture, or the fabbrica of the city, constitutes an essentially collective artifact and derives from this its characteristic features."[37] In Rossi's analytical equation, the subordinate term was always erased. With respect to the object, this process led to type; in the domain of the subject, it led to the collective dimensions of human subjectivity.

Rossi stressed the dialectic between people and their environment as a central architectural concern. He quoted Maurice Halbwachs in this regard: "'When a group is introduced into a part of space, it transforms it to its image, but at the same time, it yields and adapts itself to certain material things which resist it. It encloses itself in the framework that it has constructed. The image of the exterior environment and the stable relationships that it maintains with it pass into the realm of the idea that it has of itself.'"[38] His architecture intended to invite the collective and to facilitate the inevitable changes that members of the local culture and history would produce. It constructed a dialectical ground that sustained a collective way of life. The specific nature of that collectivity would be imprinted by its own historical context and it, in turn, would imprint the material world with its own characteristic needs and interests. An architecture that succeeded in fostering these characteristics and refusing others could aid in the maintenance and perhaps the creation of Rossi's imagined collective subject.

But Rossi also struggled with the autobiographical content of his work. Consumed by an interest in the collective, quixotically he always returned to his struggles between his "self and not-self."[39] Ironically, Rossi later returned to himself as his most important subject, the very thing that he attempted to eliminate in the early part of his career. In a 1976 publication of his work, he argued that "the repetition of characteristic personal architectural features has no special validity and correspondingly little interest. Such values are mainly of concern to the historian."[40] Yet he also recognized that "in the most recent projects general and personal tensions emerge with greater clarity."[41] Such accounts describe the kind of divisive engagement he maintained in his work, a rationalism that struggled with the irrational, an architecture of remembering and forgetting, one of permanence and change: "In any case I am increasingly convinced of what I wrote several years ago in the 'Introduction to Boullée': that in order to study the irrational it is necessary somehow to take up a rational position as observer."[42]

In the same vein, his desire for the collective might invite precisely that which has been erased or excluded—the individual, subjective, and bourgeois—and not at all the collective that Rossi intended. In light of the experiences that critics have recorded, some have argued that his work is personal, even "hermetic."

> The Architecture of the City . . . is a very private and personal text. It is the written analogue of yet another analogous process; the unconscious revelation of a potential new relationship of man to object. It anticipates the psychological subject . . . [and] nostalgically evokes the individual subject, the mythic hero-architect of humanism. . . . The potential transformation of the individual into the collective subject is left in suspension. Ambiguously, the object of the analogous city begins to define the subject once again, not so much as a humanist-hero, nor as the psychological collective, but as a complex, divided, and shattered solitary survivor, appearing before, but not withstanding, the collective will of history.[43]

While aspirations for the new in Western modernist hands had led to works that were considered cold, intellectual, and alienating, Rossi attempted to use the familiar as the basis for an architecture that could invite life and evoke memories and associations. It was an architecture intended to be meaningful. Yet, in the end, regardless of his efforts to the contrary, Rossi seemed to have made the familiar strange. He sought a timeless architecture and, as such, refused to "express the age" through his work. His assumption was that the age would express itself in his work, an architecture prepared to accept the transformations that history and life would make of it.

In contrast to Rossi's refusal, Venturi Scott Brown and Associates assumed the role of historical interpretation and used the familiar to express this, in the firm's early work, as the basis for an architecture of compromise and accommodation and, later, in a theory of architecture that would address the mediated sensibilities of late twentieth-century culture. It is this that will be considered in the next chapter.

4 VENTURI SCOTT BROWN AND ASSOCIATES

Through unconventional organization of conventional parts [the architect] . . . is able to create new meanings within the whole. If he uses convention unconventionally, if he organizes familiar things in an unfamiliar way, he is changing their contexts and he can use even cliché to gain a fresh effect. Familiar things seen in an unfamiliar context become perceptually new as well as old.

—Robert Venturi, *Complexity and Contradiction in Architecture*

Like Rossi, Robert Venturi was caught up in autobiography in his early work. In the first paragraph of his book *Complexity and Contradiction in Architecture,* for example, he declared his personal preferences for certain characteristics and historical styles of architecture: "I like complexity and contradiction in architecture. I do not like the incoherence or arbitrariness of incompetent architecture nor the precious intricacies of picturesqueness or expressionism. Instead, I speak of a complex and contradictory architecture based on the richness and ambiguity of modern experience, including that experience which is inherent in art."[1] He expanded on his preferences as the basis for laying out the agenda at the beginning of the book: "I like elements which are hybrid rather than 'pure,' compromising rather than 'clean,' distorted rather than 'straightforward,' ambiguous rather than 'articulated,' perverse as well as impersonal . . . accommodating rather than excluding. . . . I am for messy vitality over obvious unity. I include the non sequitur and proclaim the duality."[2]

This autobiographical dimension to his work, however, was later reduced both in his buildings and in his publications. While the term "I" dominated the body of the text in *Complexity and Contradiction,* "we" was used exclusively in the end section, which documents several of Venturi's projects. In addition, Venturi wrote his later book, *Learning from Las Vegas,* with coauthors, which meant that that book was dominated by the pronoun "we" and its family of related terms. Given his conviction concerning multiplicity, including the multivoiced nature of architectural practice, as well as the fact that the work of Venturi and Denise Scott Brown includes other participants, such as partners in architectural practice and coauthors in various publications, Venturi and Scott Brown prefer that, except in special cases, their architectural works be referred to as the work of Venturi Scott Brown and Associates (VSBA).[3]

The firm assumed that architectural practice was inherently complex, diverse, and plural, that is, that many people contributed to the design and production of any building. It made the same assumption about the city as a physical manifestation of complex, multiple, and diverse interests, that is, as evidence of the history and culture of individuals and local populations. The city, built up over time, could present evidence of many historical periods and changing individual and cultural interests, needs, ideas, desires, and values. Based on their study of the works of Herbert Gans, a cultural anthropologist, the architects also assumed that, while past historical epochs might have been more coherent than the present one, what seemed to be most characteristic of late twentieth-century American culture was that it contained diverse group interests and taste cultures.

The historicist assumptions VSBA made about late twentieth-century American culture were relevant for the individual subject as well, a subject that was a member of various communities faced with a multitude of oppositions and contradictions in a period of political and cultural uncertainties. These conditions had produced a new subject, one that was shaped by the new world of media and speed. This subject had developed new sensibilities that were in compliance with the new cultural forces and thus were a part of the new age. The only possible "inner peace" for the contemporary subject consisted of a tension-filled complexity based on an equilibrium of opposites.

Venturi suggested a model of equilibrium in borrowing both from T. S. Eliot (who coined the phrase "difficult poetry" to describe his own work) and from gestalt perceptual theory (which promoted the "difficult whole" or the "difficult unity") as the model of perceptual complexity. As Venturi explained, the difficult whole is "the difficult unity through inclusion rather than the easy unity through exclusion. Gestalt psychology considers a perceptual whole the result of, and yet more than, the sum of its parts. The whole is dependent on the position, number, and inherent characteristics of the parts. A complex system in Herbert A. Simon's definition includes 'a large number of parts that interact in a non-simple way.' The difficult whole in an architecture of complexity and contradiction includes multiplicity and diversity of elements in relationships that are inconsistent or among the weaker kinds perceptually."[4] The complexity of contemporary architectural interests as well as those of the individual subject and the emerging global culture could also be understood by means of this model. Under these conditions, the architect's main responsibility consisted of providing "the organization of a unique whole through conventional parts and the judicious introduction of new parts," the mix of which would appeal to diverse interests in a complex unity.[5]

Like the architecture of VSBA, the subject of the difficult unity can be understood as an aggregation of binary concepts assembled into a tense equilibrium.[6] This subject could be supported through an architecture that was, like the difficult unity of gestalt perception, an intricate equilibrium of diverse interests. This conceptual framework was sufficiently open and flexible to represent and to satisfy varying interests simultaneously. An architecture based on these ideas could become a model for similar accommodations of differences among members of society as well.

The difficult whole consisted of an array of binaries, an idea that VSBA had developed from its analyses of architecture and that was most evident in Venturi's *Complexity and Contradiction,* which is a catalog of architectural dualities. Although VSBA was concerned with the "medium degrees of multiplicity," Venturi confidently "proclaimed the duality." *Complexity and Contradiction* focused on identifying, describing, and illustrating historical examples that demonstrated relationships that were described in *Learning from Las Vegas* as "double functioning or vestigial elements, circumstantial distortions, expedient devices, eventful exceptions, exceptional diagonals, things in things, crowded or contained intricacies, linings or layerings, residual spaces, redundant spaces, ambiguities, inflections, dualities, difficult wholes, or the phenomena of both-and . . . [and relationships, such as] inclusion, inconsistency, compromise, accommodation, adaptation, superadjacency, equivalence, multiple focus, juxtaposition, or good *and* bad space."[7] As VSBA saw it, the historical reality of late twentieth-century America was characterized by competing, diverse, and plural interests, and their early conclusion was that architecture should reflect this condition. The firm used this as a framework to promote a more accommodating sensibility.

One of the most important strategies for accommodation can be found in VSBA's interpretation of the nineteenth-century concept of *poché*. Inherited from the teaching and practices of Venturi's teacher and mentor, Louis Kahn, the term referred to the spatial character recorded in walls and ceilings through such devices as niches, pilasters, and vaults.[8] Poché gave shape and character to space. The VSBA architects cited the Salk Institute to demonstrate it, pointing to the left-over spaces between the cylindrical and cubic volumes as examples (figs. 70, 71), and used "detached linings," "layers," and other spatial concepts to demonstrate the variety of possibilities that it presented (figs. 72, 73).[9] Poché was cited in *Complexity and Contradiction* in the discussions pertaining to the relationships between the outside and the inside. The idea frequently resurfaced in the text in relation to what has been called the "struggle between the interior requirements of a building and those of its exterior envelope."[10] The idea of poché referred to the spatial impressions in and accommodations by the mass of the wall. If designed properly, Venturi wrote, the exterior wall made it possible to "induce simultaneous awareness of what is significant on either side. An in-between space in this sense provided the common ground where conflicting polarities can

Figure 70. Louis I. Kahn, model, Salk Institute Community Center, La Jolla, California, 1959–65 (unbuilt). (Photo copyright © 1977, courtesy of Louis I. Kahn Collection, University of Pennsylvania and Pennsylvania Historical and Museum Commission)

again become twin phenomena" and achieved the difficult unity of two conflicting conditions, thus demonstrating compromise and accommodation while also presenting a late-twentieth-century version of transparency.[11]

Following the example of Kahn, VSBA also inverted the nineteenth-century idea of poché from solid to void, conceiving it as a new spatial condition, a "residual space" that was "always leftover, inflected toward something more important beyond itself."[12] Unlike modern architecture that constantly deferred to the efficient use of material and construction practices and produced only flat planes and generally rectangular volumes, VSBA's use of residual space would return the possibility of spatial shape and hierarchy to architecture. Space could now be "charged" with the valences that differentiated primary from secondary spaces.

Residual space proved valuable to architecture because it permitted the articulation of more than the simple abstractions of lines, planes, and volumes that modern construction practices, driven primarily by economic choices, had adopted.[13] Architecture did not have to be limited to the simple geometries sympathetic to such practices and could, through such ideas and practices as poché, offer a much richer array of spatial experiences. The study of the in-between provided VSBA with the means of returning to what it considered a rich premodern architecture. This abundance came from the

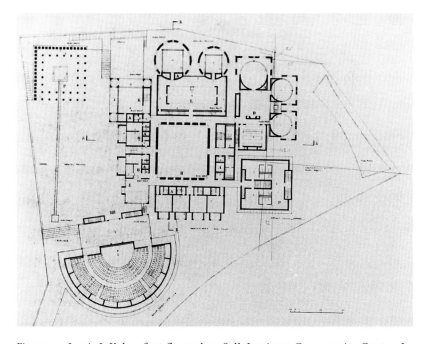

Figure 71. Louis I. Kahn, first-floor plan, Salk Institute Community Center, La Jolla, California, 1959–65 (unbuilt). (Photo copyright © 1977, courtesy of Louis I. Kahn Collection, University of Pennsylvania and Pennsylvania Historical and Museum Commission)

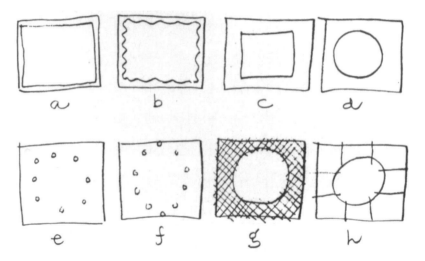

Figure 72. Venturi Scott Brown and Associates, plan diagrams. (Courtesy Venturi Scott Brown and Associates)

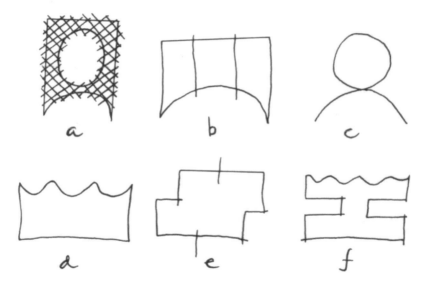

Figure 73. Venturi Scott Brown and Associates, facade diagrams. (Courtesy Venturi Scott Brown and Associates)

array of architectural spaces—and the relationships among them—that premodern construction practices offered.

Spatial hierarchy, inflection, and accommodation are evident in VSBA's own architecture, most readily in the Vanna Venturi House, a house designed in 1963 for Robert Venturi's mother in Chestnut Hill, Pennsylvania (figs. 74–78).[14] The Vanna Venturi House is a relatively simple little house filled with varied and complex architectural references, changes in scale, and deformations that represent various taste cultures and that embody accommodations and compromises.[15] Venturi argues that these deformations are made to a neoclassical base:

> This almost Palladian rigidity and symmetry is distorted, however, to accommodate the particular needs of the spaces: the kitchen on the right, for instance, varies from the bedroom on the left.
>
> A more violent kind of accommodation occurs within the central core itself. Two vertical elements—the fireplace/chimney and the stair—compete, as it were, for central position. And each of these elements, one essentially solid, the other essentially void, compromises in its shape and position—that is, inflects—toward the other to make a unity of the duality of the central core they constitute. . . . Toward the front, it is shaped by a diagonal wall accommodating the also important and unique directional needs of the entrance space. . . . The stair, considered as an element alone in its awkward residual space, is bad; in relation to its position in a hierarchy of uses and spaces, however, it is a fragment appropriately accommodating a complex and contradictory whole, and as such it is good.[16]

Other accommodations occur throughout the house. As Scully describes it, "So Venturi tries loosening up the kitchen, and then moves on in that rhythm to unite the whole thing; working with circles to resonate off the entrance arc, the stair coming alive, the two bedrooms adjusting to the circulation and each other."[17]

Guild House in Philadelphia (1960–63) demonstrated other accommodations (figs. 79, 80). At the urban scale, the building is intended to be contextual and to accept, for the most part, the local architecture as the basis for its materials, construction, and proportions. For example, it employs brick

Figure 74. Venturi and Rauch, Vanna Venturi House, Chestnut Hill, Pennsylvania, 1961–64. (Photo by Rollin La France, courtesy Venturi Scott Brown and Associates)

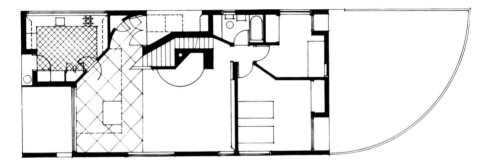

Figure 75. Venturi and Rauch, first-floor plan, Vanna Venturi House, Chestnut Hill, Pennsylvania, 1961–64. (Courtesy Venturi Scott Brown and Associates)

Figure 76. Venturi and Rauch, rear view, Vanna Venturi House, Chestnut Hill, Pennsylvania, 1961–64. (Photo by Rollin La France, courtesy Venturi Scott Brown and Associates)

Figure 77. Venturi and Rauch, interior, Vanna Venturi House, Chestnut Hill, Pennsylvania, 1961–64. (Photo by Rollin La France, courtesy Venturi Scott Brown and Associates)

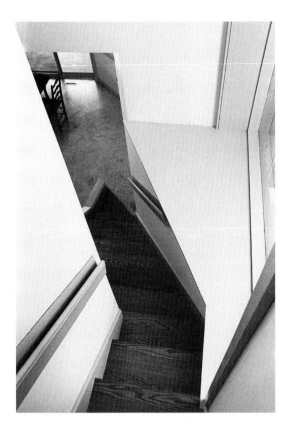

Figure 78. Venturi and
Rauch, view of stairs,
Vanna Venturi House,
Chestnut Hill, Pennsyl-
vania, 1961–64. (Photo
by Rollin La France,
courtesy Venturi Scott
Brown and Associates)

and uses double-hung windows. The building also addresses a public scale, best represented by its rectangular facade—designed as a screen—with a giant arch at the top as a symbol of entrance and a large granite column at the base supporting a sign displaying the name of the building. The white base with its glazed tiles and the exaggerated lettering attached to the second-floor balustrade were borrowed from supermarket aesthetics (figs. 81, 82).[18] The plan repeats the angled interior walls of the Vanna Venturi House, continuing one of the architectural means of expressing compromise. These and other design choices accommodated the diversity of expectations and interests of the new era, in the manner in which VSBA conceived of these. Poché, therefore, more or less resolved the split condition that enabled architecture to accommodate differences. Accommodation practices sustained the objective of, and made possible, the difficult whole. Venturi wrote, "These complex combinations do not achieve the easy harmony of a few motifs based on exclusion—based, that is, on 'less is more.' Instead, they achieve the difficult unity of a medium number of diverse parts based on inclusion and on acknowledgment of the diversity of experience."[19] The model of the difficult whole, in turn, could act as a model of the plural culture of diverse interests that architecture had to accommodate.

The early projects of VSBA tended to serve as sites for the promotion and

Figure 79. Venturi and Rauch, Cope and Lippincott, Associated Architects, Guild House, Philadelphia, Pennsylvania, 1960–63. (Photo by Skomark Associates, courtesy Venturi Scott Brown and Associates)

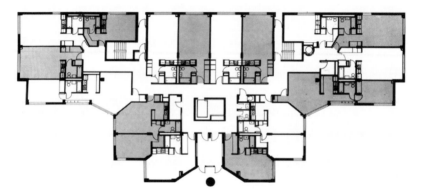

Figure 80. Venturi and Rauch, Cope and Lippincott, Associated Architects, first-floor plan, Guild House, Philadelphia, Pennsylvania, 1960–63. (Courtesy Venturi Scott Brown and Associates)

embodiment of the accommodation of complexities and contradictions. The use of familiar types and the sympathetic response to local contexts made this possible. An architecture based on this combination would be valid and would contribute to "inner peace . . . [achieved through] a tension among contradictions and uncertainties."[20]

As a device, poché primarily demonstrated accommodation. But accommodation was not merely a spatial condition. More significant, it manifested a historical and cultural condition. In terms of history, VSBA depended on a framework of past and present similar to the one in Le Corbusier's and Aldo Rossi's work. The primary difference, however, is that VSBA's work depended on a familiar background upon which it would represent the new, a practice

Figure 81. Venturi and Rauch, Cope and Lippincott, Associated Architects, entrance, Guild House, Philadelphia, Pennsylvania, 1960–63. (Courtesy Venturi Scott Brown and Associates)

Figure 82. Venturi and Rauch, Cope and Lippincott, Associated Architects, detail, Guild House, Philadelphia, Pennsylvania, 1960–63. (Photo by Skomark Associates, courtesy Venturi Scott Brown and Associates)

that contrasts sharply with Rossi's. This background was based on typical and vernacular buildings and elements like Rossi's and not, as in Le Corbusier's work, on an abstraction of classical spaces and contemporary forms.

We can understand the specific nature of VSBA's Guild House project better by examining the use of the term "familiar."[21] In describing the windows of Guild House, for example, VSBA states that they "look familiar; they *look like,* as well as *are,* windows, and in this respect their use is explicitly symbolic. But like all effective symbolic images, they are intended to look familiar and unfamiliar. They are the conventional element used slightly unconventionally. Like the subject matter of Pop Art they are commonplace elements made uncommon through distortion in shape (slight), changing scale (they are much bigger than normal double-hung windows), and changes in context (double-hung windows in perhaps high-fashion building)."[22] The firm's theoretical position was fundamentally structured along the lines of the opposition of the familiar and the unfamiliar. As expressed in the epigraph for this chapter, VSBA assumed that the architect was "able to create new meanings within the whole. If he uses convention unconventionally, if he organizes familiar things in an unfamiliar way, he is changing their contexts and he can use even cliché to gain a fresh effect. Familiar things seen in an unfamiliar context become perceptually new as well as old."[23] This could be achieved by "seeing familiar things in an unfamiliar way and from unexpected points of view."[24] The same conclusions can be drawn from an examination of VSBA's use of associated terms, often used as synonyms, such as "ordinary," "common," "everyday," and "conventional," as when Venturi quotes Wordsworth that "ordinary things should be presented to the mind in an unusual aspect."[25]

The firm's purpose in advocating the familiar stemmed from the associations that it could provoke. The use of conventional elements in ordinary architecture, "be they dumb doorknobs or the familiar forms of existing construction systems—evokes associations from past experience."[26] Ultimately, the architects argue for an architecture based on association, claiming that "an architecture that depends on association in its perception depends on association in its creation."[27] In their work, this showed up in the ornament in Guild House, which depended on explicit associations: "it looks like what it is not only because of what it is but also because of what it reminds you of . . . with its explicit, almost heraldic, associations."[28]

The concepts of type and the typical, both of which figured significantly in the concept of the familiar, operated at several scales. Broad typologies, ranging from the basilican and centralized church forms to multiple-unit housing, existed at the level of the building. At the scale of human beings, typological elements included windows, doors, and rooms as well as their conventional ornamental treatment. At levels above the building, these included urban and regional types, including the Las Vegas Strip as the most extreme example of a typical development along a major thoroughfare.

Types were important to VSBA, because of their familiarity and their ability to evoke associations. The familiar could act as a foil, as background, for the expression of the new age. For VSBA, like some of its modernist progenitors, the "new" was unfamiliar: the new landscape, the new scales, the new speeds, the new spaces and forms brought on by modern transportation, especially the automobile. These brought with them new sensibilities and new meanings. In VSBA's work the familiar/unfamiliar framework made it possible to evoke new meanings to satisfy new sensibilities.

According to VSBA, new subjects had interests in the visual tensions that pop artists presented, and they took advantage of this art to propose a parallel architecture. "Pop artists used unusual juxtapositions of everyday objects in tense and vivid plays between old and new associations to flout the everyday interdependence of context and meaning, giving us a new interpretation of twentieth-century cultural artifacts."[29]

The architecture of VSBA attempted to deconstruct the relationship between context and meaning in order to juxtapose the familiar and the unfamiliar. In addition, the firm used certain visual techniques to disrupt habits of vision, to challenge enculturated practices of seeing. In Guild House, for example, the architects attempted "to disturb the habitual perception of distance through perspective."[30]

The new, however, depended on types and typical elements. The National Football Hall of Fame project (1967, unbuilt), for example, included a main space that was covered by a barrel vault, a spatial form that, according to VSBA, had associations with sacred spaces, such as basilicas. They considered it an appropriate architectural element for this building because of the heroic, indeed sacred proportions that Americans ascribed to their athletes.

At the scale of windows and doorknobs the associations are also effective on the level of the body, as in the stairs, the disproportionate windows, and the segmental barrel vault in the Vanna Venturi House. The manipulation of scale and context, as well as the use of elements with almost archetypal associations, added a sense of aesthetic tension that held the potential for new meaning.

At levels above human scale, however, the body lost its status as a means of measurement, proportion, and scale: "The body sensations of speed are few in a car. We depend upon vision for our perception of speed."[31] At the scale of the automobile, for example, new spaces and forms became apparent: the block, the city, and the region became important issues. Signs began to take over the landscape as new subjects moved toward the almost exclusive domain of the eye.

There is a strong visual focus in VSBA's work already evident in *Complex-*

ity and Contradiction, which was a treatise on formal aspects of architecture largely conceived through the visual principles of gestalt psychology. The lessons VSBA learned from Las Vegas were also explicitly visual in nature and led eventually to the firm's declaration of an architecture of signs.

> We shall emphasize image . . . in asserting that architecture depends in its perception and creation on past experience and emotional association and that these symbolic and representational elements may often be contradictory to the form, structure, and program with which they combine in the same building. We shall survey this contradiction in its two main manifestations:
>
> 1. Where the architectural systems of space, structure, and program are submerged and distorted by an overall symbolic form. This kind of building-becoming-sculpture we call the *duck.* . . .
>
> 2. Where systems of space and structure are directly at the service of program, and ornament is applied independently of them. This we call the *decorated shed.* . . .
>
> The duck is the special building that *is* a symbol; the decorated shed is the conventional shelter that *applies* symbols.[32]

The sign in the duck modified or distorted the otherwise honest, simple, and straightforward construction and form of a building, to which they referred as a "shed" (figs. 83, 84). The sign in the decorated shed was applied or attached and hence did not deform the shed. In an architecture of the decorated shed, the sign function became separated from the sheltering function.

VSBA argued that, given the pragmatic and economic factors of architectural practice in the late twentieth century, the decorated shed became the only appropriate response. The duck was fine, even appropriate for other historical moments, but not today. The architects' commitment to this idea is evident in most of their work. In the Vanna Venturi House, for example, the front facade extended vertically beyond the roof and laterally beyond the side walls to make its screen-like character explicit.[33] Guild House was also designed as a decorated shed. The more extreme possibilities are demonstrated in the National Football Hall of Fame Project and the BASCO Showroom (1971) (figs. 85–87).

VSBA considered it important for architecture to retrieve its capacity to carry signs—a capacity that modernism had attempted to eliminate—in order to communicate with popular taste and culture, in large part because (as scholarship and research suggested) people basically perceived the world in terms of signs and symbols.[34] Architecture could not overlook the visual interest in seeing the world in such a way if it was to appeal to popular taste. Such an interest should not have been resisted or criticized, as modernists had done, but rather should have been included as one of the many ways in which diverse interests could be accommodated in architecture. Given the

Figure 83. "The Duck" (Courtesy Venturi Scott Brown and Associates)

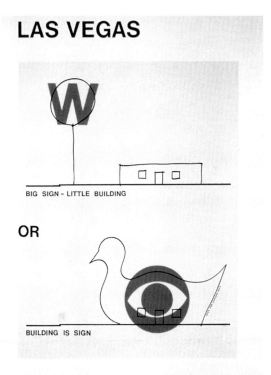

Figure 84. Venturi Scott Brown and Associates, drawings, "The Duck and the Decorated Shed." (Courtesy Venturi Scott Brown and Associates)

new sensibilities, the most appropriate architecture was "a complex and contradictory . . . [one] based on the richness and ambiguity of modern experience."[35] *Complexity and Contradiction* served as a handbook of conditions by means of which one could practice such an architecture.

VSBA consistently argued in the 1970s for a "populist" architecture, that is, one in which signs that would be commonly understood should be popular, reassuring, and easily legible.[36] The firm argued that buildings "ought to be regarded as communications devices employing well-known and easily understood 'codes.'"[37] The architect should "communicate to his public through popularly established conventions."[38] This is manifested, for example, in Guild House's common and contextual aspects and the references to the shingle-style houses of the northeast in the facade of the Vanna Venturi House.

At the same time that architecture grounded itself in the familiar, however, it had to take into consideration the new sensibilities that arose in the "chaotic reality"[39] of an age steeped in what Michael Crosbie calls "ambiguity and pluralism."[40] An architecture appropriate to this age would complement and promote such diversity as well as the new sensibilities of accommodation that such a culture would require in order to maintain itself in the new and contemporary equilibrium; as Crosbie writes, a "valid architecture evokes many levels of meaning and combinations of focus: its space and its elements become readable and workable in several ways at once."[41] In order to survive and flourish in an age of ambiguity and pluralism, VSBA argued that architects had to learn to be receptive to a diversity of client tastes. In her preface to the revised edition of *Learning from Las Vegas,* for example, Denise Scott Brown stated that architects "should learn to reassess the role

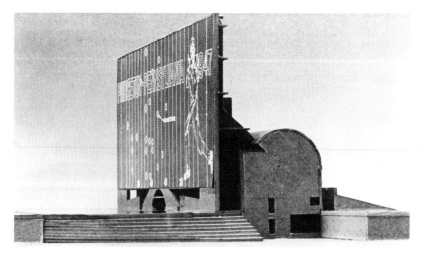

Figure 85. Venturi Scott Brown and Associates, model, National Football Hall of Fame competition entry, Rutgers University, New Brunswick, New Jersey, 1967. (Courtesy Venturi Scott Brown and Associates)

Figure 86. Venturi Scott Brown and Associates, BASCO Showroom, Bristol Township, Pennsylvania, 1971. (Photo by Tom Bernard, courtesy Venturi Scott Brown and Associates)

Figure 87. Venturi Scott Brown and Associates, detail, BASCO Showroom, Bristol Township, Pennsylvania, 1971. (Photo by Tom Bernard, courtesy Venturi Scott Brown and Associates)

of symbolism in architecture, and, in the process, to learn a new receptivity to the tastes and values of other people and a new modesty in our designs and in our perception of our role as architects in society. Architecture for the last quarter of our century should be socially less coercive and aesthetically more vital than the striving and bombastic buildings of our recent past."[42]

Despite the avowedly populist stance of VSBA, however, some observers criticized its architecture as elitist.[43] They considered it an architecture "which is arcane, and which, though it is accommodating to the needs of the client, is ultimately addressed to those who understand and love architecture for itself."[44] The Vanna Venturi House, for example, contains architectural devices and references that reflect Venturi's considerable knowledge of architectural history as well as evidence of the historical styles that he preferred, as in the Palladian-like window on the second floor in the rear, the interior molding on the exterior, and the baroque gesture of the split facade. Characterized as "mannerized commentaries on earlier architecture,"[45] its "manipulation of quotations required an in-crowd of *savants* for its full communicative effect."[46] It was even considered highly and idiosyncratically personal.[47]

In a review of a presentation that Venturi made at the Architectural Association in May 1978, for example, a critic stated that "Venturi showed a number of recent projects whose . . . neutral structures were ornamented with 'incorrect' orders and other incongruous details. Who but other architects 'in the know' were the object of these exercises? . . . Venturi's wit seems to be aimed solely at his fellow architects. The semiological intention of these projects is clearly not to provide the client with what he wants (though an essential part of the joke is that they do so *faute de mieux*), but to draw attention to the absurdity of popular taste."[48] Although correct, this criticism failed to consider the full dimensions of the plurality that VSBA proposed. Given its constant insistence on inclusivity, the firm intended its work to serve different interests in architecture, including those concerned with the history of architecture and its "disciplinary" conditions. It might even include those who respect the dexterity or genius that the architects demonstrated in their work, especially their associations. Although this position would be considered complicitous by some, such inclusivity was endemic to their work.

Critics also suspected VSBA of insincerity in its interest in the tastes of its clients. The gold anodized TV antenna on Guild House, for example, was said to make a "disturbing comment on the life of the aged"; it received serious criticism based on this perspective that called into question VSBA's actual commitment to popular taste (fig. 88).[49] This building was described as outrageous, annoying, and offensive.[50] The Vanna Venturi House was originally ignored or scorned.[51] The firm's later strip malls were called theatrical and scenographic.[52] In fact, VSBA was often criticized for the familiar elements or conditions that were included in its work.

Receptivity to the tastes and values of other people required VSBA to set aside its architects' own interests or at least not to let them interfere in serving the needs of the client. Yet, as Colquhoun points out, this practice is difficult because, "when an architect is called in to provide the 'architecture,' he is expected to share the objectives and taste of the client and to act merely as his agent. . . . In order to assume the role of 'servant' to society, the modern architect must submit to a self-denying ordinance and play a game of 'let's pretend.'"[53]

The concept of the decorated shed only underscored these critics' reservations. Some found the possibility of the complete separation between sign and substance disturbing. Colquhoun even argued that "[n]o theory of meaning in architecture can make sense unless it seeks to establish a relation between the general concept of a building and its parts, or between its ornament and its structural and spatial scheme."[54] For these observers, the separation in the decorated shed attacked the very epicenter of the architectural act; the disturbing character of this separation centered precisely on the fact that it was a wholly unbridgeable split. The space in between was haunted by the possibility that the assumed relationships between sign and substance were in fact arbitrary: the connections were at least partially constructed. This possibility even threatened nihilism: the world might not be transparent, but rather opaque, inaccessible, and unknowable. The early modernist interest in transparency would be impossible if this were true.

The gap between sign and substance created by the decorated shed sug-

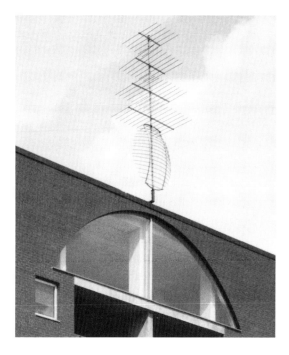

Figure 88. Venturi and Rauch, Cope and Lippincott, Associated Architects, detail of antenna, Guild House, Philadelphia, Pennsylvania, 1960–63. (Photo by William Watkins, courtesy Venturi Scott Brown and Associates)

gested an architecture without the capacity to reveal what was within or beyond; it masked and masqueraded. In addition, it was an architecture that was eminently adaptive: the sign on the shed changed whenever the function it signified changed. One of the primary criticisms of the concept suggested that an architecture of the decorated shed would reduce the role of the architect to that of a mere "purveyor of signs."[55] In terms of the culture, an architecture of signs would reflect a superficial and disconnected array of actors about whom nothing could ever be certain.

In the hands of VSBA, signs have more often than not been explicit. In applying the model of the decorated shed to the subject, however, we engage the possibility of illusory subjects, actors, and performances. The most radical of these subjects are never what they seem and they can adapt at will; like the signs on any shed, the masks of performances can be changed as well. This bespeaks the opposite of the transparent world—that is, a world in which the subject could see everything honestly expressed and nothing concealed—that American architects had sought at the turn of the nineteenth century. It implies a world of illusions, a world that many have feared and criticized for decades.[56] If this is the object that satisfied the interests of the contemporary subject, it implied as well an architectural interest that would overturn the consensual interest in transparency and replace it with a world in which there are only performances.

The tensions of complexity that VSBA promoted in *Complexity and Contradiction* were based on the already tenuous unity of the difficult whole. Venturi described this as an "inherent sense of unity not far from the surface. It is not the obvious or easy unity derived from the dominant binder or the motival order of simpler, less contradictory compositions, but that derived from a complex and illusive order of the difficult whole. It is the taut composition which contains contrapuntal relationships, equal combinations, inflected fragments, and acknowledged dualities."[57] These compositions supported a tenuous equilibrium derived from the strength of the difficult whole, which, as August Heckscher put it, "maintains, but only just maintains, a control over the clashing elements which compose it. Chaos is very near; its nearness, but its avoidance gives . . . force."[58] One suspects that the same can be said about the imagined societies and, to a degree, the subjects of VSBA's work.

The appropriate architecture (as VSBA regarded it, "valid" architecture) for this new era was to be a difficult whole based on the familiar and imbued with contradictions and inconsistencies operating on many levels simultaneously. Familiar elements in new contexts would be relevant to the practice of architecture as well as to the cultures and clients it served. The society, subjects, and objects of an age of plural and diverse interests could be imagined as consisting of "seemingly dissimilar things . . . [existing] side by side" held together in an equilibrium that was the basis for "inner peace."[59]

CONCLUSION

The four architects or firms whose work we have examined in the foregoing chapters have all demonstrated a concern for the familiar and the unfamiliar. This framework has helped us to uncover some of the experiences that these architects have imagined for their subjects. In comparing their subjects, however, we should keep in mind that the texts we have examined are early works, done at a relatively young age. At times, the texts reflect that youthfulness; the architects' later works often demonstrate more mature and well-developed perspectives. In addition, the genres of writing are quite different. While Wright's writings are sermon-like and reflect his religious upbringing, Le Corbusier writes like a pamphleteer, one who publishes proclamations as a means of provocation. By comparison, Rossi and VSBA's texts are more conventionally written in the styles of research and scholarship, respectively.

The works of all four can be understood as reflecting something familiar and something new or strange, which seems to corroborate the framework that Freud established for the uncanny: what is familiar is somehow tied to what is not. They each included the familiar and the unfamiliar in their thoughts about architecture. What are familiar in Wright's work are certain architectural features (such as the fireplace nook) that he continued to use in many of his earliest works and certain functional relationships and expectations. For example, although free-flowing space is a primary condition, certain levels of privacy are still maintained: there are doors to the bedrooms and bathrooms; the kitchen is segregated from the dining room. There are similar reinforcements about issues of publicity and privacy in Le Corbusier's work. Thus, certain conventional expectations and relationships are satisfied. What is strange about VSBA's work is precisely what Colquhoun criticized, that is, the possibility of the loss of the architectural capacity or responsibility to embody meaning. As for Rossi, critics were quick to point to the strange experience that his work evoked. With certain cautions, we can use some of the observations we have made as the basis for addressing some additional issues.

Wright and Le Corbusier had intentions that were essentially the reverse of those of the later architects. They dedicated their architecture to the new or the unfamiliar. Both men agreed substantially on the broad historicist assumption that Western culture had moved into a new era and that it was the architect's responsibility to understand and to express that condition in his or her architecture. Both attempted to make the new appear to us in their work in order to make it familiar. But the project of using architecture to express the new became, for many architects in the second half of the century, alienating and irrelevant. In contrast to early modernist attempts to orient subjects in this manner, therefore, Rossi and VSBA based their work on the familiar, assuming that it would ground architecture in ways that would be meaningful. The familiar could also be used as the background for other issues, including the appearance of life, as in the work of Rossi, or the enactment of compromise and accommodation, as in the early work of VSBA.

The differences between the earlier architects and the later practitioners are also evident in their assumptions about the modes of experience that their subjects enjoyed, especially vision and sensations of the body. In the early half of the century, for example, the new experiences provided by transportation—the train, airplane, dirigible, and automobile—as well as new technologies—the camera, the microscope, the X ray—extended human movement and vision. The eye, as if disembodied, could now observe the world from above or at high rates of speed. It could also travel inside the human body, suggesting and perhaps manifesting a desire to make visible that which is invisible, to see beyond, beneath, and through. Cubism suggested some of the same interests. As Giedion claimed, "we are no longer limited to seeing objects from the distances normal for earth-bound animals. The bird's-eye view has opened up to us whole new aspects of the world. Such new modes of perception carry with them new feelings which the artist must formulate."[1]

These technological inventions introduced subjects to experiences of space and time that were altogether unfamiliar outside conventional experiences and, in fact, impossible on a broad scale before the modern era. They presented new spaces outside the norm, disengaged from the historical limitations of gravity and human perception. Each promoted a new way of seeing and favored a new visual interest, a new "desire of our eyes" that resulted from seeing in new ways, at new scales and distances, and at new speeds. Because of these new techniques and the desires they are alleged to have produced, some observers maintained that the arts, including architecture, had to be reconfigured if they were to be historically relevant. For Giedion and others, historical relevance pertained to the subject as well; an architecture appropriate to the age made it possible "to discover harmonies between our own inner states and our surroundings."[2]

Artists were already exploring these issues at the beginning of the century by attempting to depict new ways of seeing. While the tradition of perspective had governed artistic habits of and assumptions about seeing ever since the Renaissance, artists in the first quarter of the twentieth century were exploring simultaneous space-time conditions as one means of correspondence with the age.[3] As Giedion wrote,

> [I]n modern art, for the first time since the Renaissance, a new conception of space leads to a self-conscious enlargement of our ways of perceiving space. . . . The cubists did not seek to reproduce the appearance of objects from one vantage point; they went round them, tried to lay hold of their internal constitution. They sought to extend the scale of feeling, just as contemporary science extends its descriptions to cover new levels of material phenomena.
>
> Cubism breaks with Renaissance perspective. It views objects relatively: that is, from several points of view, no one of which has exclusive authority. And in so dissecting objects it sees them simultaneously from all sides— from above and below, from inside and outside. It goes around and into its objects.[4]

Beginning in the late 1910s, Le Corbusier attempted to present another version of simultaneity in his architecture and in his paintings.[5] He demonstrated the tension of spaces and forms in a cubist or, in his terms, purist interpenetration that he assumed expressed new and appropriate ways of seeing. These new modes involved the qualities of transparency and simultaneity,[6] including the disembodied spaces of abstraction, the mental spaces of geometry and mathematics, and the complexities of Einsteinian space-time. They were the primary means by which architecture attempted to align itself with "our inner states."

For Wright, the liberation of the subject became possible by promoting openness, honesty, and truthfulness, suggesting the moral dimension to his work. If fully transparent, the world could be known and subjects would know their location in space and time. In addition, the values used in shaping the material world would be clear and self-evident and would promote a similar set of values among those who experienced this kind of work. Subjects would gain the pleasures associated with these experiences.

In response to the alienation that many associated with late modernist work in the 1960s, however, some architects began to seek ways in which their work could be more meaningful—that is, more familiar—by using conventional, typical, or common forms, spaces, and images. This is clearest, perhaps, in the study of signs, as in the work of Rossi and VSBA, which emerged as a dominant focus of theoretical discourse in the 1960s and 1970s. This interest was part of a long-standing tradition in architecture, including the nineteenth-century *architecture parlante* and the twentieth-century concept that form follows function. The phrase *architecture parlante* was based on the French verb *parler,* "to speak," and thus assumed a capacity in architecture to "speak" to a subject who could "read" architecture. This form of architectural experience is evident in a long span of work, from the sculpture and painting programs in Gothic cathedrals to the revolutionary architecture of Ledoux, whose works suggested their purpose.[7] The parlante tradition reached its height in the nineteenth century as a convention in which certain historical styles became associated with functional types, such as the use of the Gothic style for religious and university buildings and the Greco-Roman style for banks and museums. The later stages of the parlante tradition are evident in the modernist assertion that form was to follow function. This assumption, however, was coupled by the replacement of styles with attention to modern materials, spaces, and construction practices. Late twentieth-century interest in semiotics, or the study of signs, continued the interest in and assumptions about a subject who reads architecture for the meanings that it represents, as in signs of life, of the collective, of the present, or of timelessness, according to different architects.

While there was much attention paid to vision throughout the twentieth century, there was also interest in the body. In certain early modernist work, the body became the basis of new and liberating experiences. According to Choay, Le Corbusier and Wright both insisted that "architecture must be walked through, traversed."[8] In fact, movement was a central concern in modernism.[9] For some critics, it expressed the defining condition of the new era. In discussing the Administrative Office Building of the 1914 Werkbund exhibition, by Walter Gropius and Adolf Meyer, for example, Richard Sennett wrote that "your eyes move inside to outside, outside to inside. . . . [T]o understand how the stairs feel you have to walk them; the door, so oddly not a barrier, invites you to enter. And this invitation to move makes again a more complicated picture than the open window of the past. . . . Gropius, Mies van der Rohe, and Marcel Breuer . . . wanted to make spaces that create a special kind of coherence due to the sequence of movement, movement through space binding person to building. Inside and outside, room and room, are unified—a unity we start to experience the moment our bodies begin to move."[10] For many, especially modernist spokespersons like Giedion, change and dynamics constituted the essence of the new age, the single condition that differentiated it from the past. The movement of the body as well as the movement offered by automobiles, trains, boats, and planes offered new body experiences that became a new focus of pleasure and aesthetics.

There are aspects of the body other than its movement in space, however, and VSBA's and Rossi's advocacy of familiar types suggests some of these. For example, the use of types already assumes certain body experiences; types contain spaces and other conditions that are familiar and which the body "remembers." Subjects remember the sizes, dimensions, and proportions in typical spaces that, in turn, can be used to evoke memories and associations. Body memory is, for some, almost palpable: Gaston Bachelard suggests this when he recalls a return visit to his childhood home.[11] VSBA makes this point in relation to its National Football Hall of Fame Building project, which consisted of a billboard attached to a barrel-vaulted space. The architects described the vaulted space as sacred because of its associations with the spatial conditions of historical religious architecture. VSBA also associated certain experiences with typical spaces and adopted the idea of poché, a concept that suggests not only visual conditions but also spatial memories; poché was a means of defining and composing spaces to inform subjects, consciously or not, of their relative importance and hierarchy.[12] In addition, there were specific issues of presence—of physicality—that certain architects considered essential to the experience of architecture; experiences of well-being could be evoked, for example, by everything from the sense of enclosure to the sense of the warmth of materials and the tactile experience of textures.

While there was much attention paid to vision and visuality at the end of the twentieth century, much of the discussion focused on the reduction to the optical. Some critics argued this was a consequence of media and new technologies and that architecture had to address the problem of "the slow slide of architecture (and just about everything else that is slow, physical, natural and real) into the world of television."[13] One of the responses to counteract increasing attention to media was an increase in attention to the body.[14]

The body became an important issue in late twentieth-century architectural discourse. Some architects and critics called on its formal properties as the basis for a return to figuration.[15] The clearest example of this in the work we have examined is that of the body in the plan of the San Cataldo Cemetery at Modena, an autobiographical representation of Rossi's own body experience after an automobile accident; although Rossi does not resort to the figure of the body often in his work, he uses a quasi-anthropomorphic composition in the plan of the school at Fagnano Olona. Others employed the body metaphorically. In Anthony Vidler's essay "The Building in Pain," for example, the author compared the classical body to the deconstructivist architecture in the late twentieth century.[16] He compared the whole, healthy, ideal male body—a body not unlike that of the "Vitruvian man"—to the work of Coop Himmelblau and Frank Gehry.[17] From this comparison, he concluded that the contemporary "body" of architecture was in pain.

Other observers, however, criticized the use of the body in figural or representational ways. This criticism often expresses concern about the loss of the body, its representation acting as a sign of the disappearance of direct, kinesthetic, and presenced experience. This is the basis, in part, for Robert McAnulty's criticism of Perez-Gomez's call for a return to figuration.[18] McAnulty cited the work of Diller and Scofidio as an example of a practice that went beyond the formal and visual characteristics of the body to engage in a critical examination of the body's cultural construction.

The disagreements among the different schools of thought raised questions about presence and representation in architecture. Just as Colquhoun voiced concerns about the relationship between sign and substance in VSBA's work or others interpreted this as a problem of the relationship between body and image, many critics and philosophers were concerned with identifying any preferred mode of experience or about the radical separation between the two.[19] For Wright and Le Corbusier, certainly, there was a clear need to experience architecture in real space and time instead of merely in drawings, models, and photographs. They assumed that a certain dimension of presence, like the movement and weight of the body, served as a means of expressing or accommodating the new. The same is not clear, however, in the work of VSBA and Rossi, whose acceptance or denial of signs suggests that certain assumptions about the nature of the subject had changed; there was less conscious concern for presence than for signs of life.

Although we have maintained some categorical separation between the eye and the body, these modes of experience are not independent of one another. Each affects the other in very complex ways. In his "Note to the Second Edition" of *Complexity and Contradiction,* Vincent Scully stated:

> There is no way to separate form from meaning; one cannot exist without the other. There can only be different critical assessments of the major ways through which form transmits meaning to the viewer: through empathy, said the nineteenth century, it embodies it; through the recognition of signs, say the linguists, it conveys it. Each side would agree that the relevant function-ing agent in this process of the human brain is the memory: empathy and the identification of signs are both learned responses, the result of specific cultural experiences. The two modes of knowing and of deriving meaning from outside reality complement each other and are both at work in varying degrees in the shaping and the perception of all works of art.[20]

The relationships between eye, body, and memory are more complex than we can describe here. The eye can activate the body, an experience that sug-gests at least the possibility of correspondence between these modes.[21]

The framework of the familiar and the unfamiliar is similarly problem-atic. Although helpful in uncovering certain aspects of the imagined subject, the framework—already complicated by Freud's claims in his examination of the uncanny, as we suggested above—should be used with certain cau-tions. There are several possible relationships between subjects and objects—as is evidenced in language—regarding proportion and projection.

One of the clearest examples of subject-object correspondence occurs in language. Many of the terms used to describe architecture are also used to describe parts of the human body. In Russell Sturgis's *Dictionary of Architec-ture and Building,* published in 1901–2, for example, there are over nine hun-dred such terms, for example, faces (facades), elbows, knees, eyes (oculi), eyebrows.[22] Architecture is full of eyes, and the city is full of faces. Figure, scale, and proportion can also be understood as other examples of the same interest. Through proportion, the dimensional relationships among the parts of the human body are assumed to correlate with relationships among parts of objects; when subjects recognize or sense this correlation, they find the objects pleasing. Through scale, subjects locate themselves in the world: they can tell distances, measure space, and orient themselves, all of which should be included in the pleasures of architecture.[23] Henri Lefebvre corrob-orates this by arguing that "one . . . relates oneself to space, situates oneself in space. One confronts both an immediacy and an objectivity of one's own. One places oneself at the centre, designates oneself, measures oneself, and uses oneself as a measure."[24] By means of these strategies of design, the world looks like us (it acts as a mirror) or, as in Giedion's case, it mirrors our inner states.

An aesthetics developed along the lines of the shape and dimension of the human body assumes that the purpose of architecture is to satisfy the need for identification—subject-object correlations—and that this is the means by which it should do so. For some this is an acceptable human interest, but for others it obscures alternate purposes that architecture could serve. In order to separate themselves from the past, therefore, many architects at the turn of the century developed new models of the body focused on some of its other dimensions as the source for a new and appropriate aesthetics. They did so by focusing on visceral and kinesthetic experiences, realms of bodily experience that did not rely solely on the visual properties of objects, since radical thinkers had discredited visual preferences as the basis for the taste culture of the aristocracy. Classical visual preferences were aligned with oppression and class culture.

The interest in transparency, by contrast, suggests a framework for subject-object correlations that does not depend on language or the classical agenda. It goes beyond the formal characteristics of the body to situate itself on the level of emotions, values, and personal characteristics. Thoreau's argument that the nature of architectural beauty depended on the character of the indweller, coupled with Whitman's ideal of "just as you . . . so I," offer us some measure of this bodiless sensibility. As Philip Fisher writes, "In this aesthetics of identity each person becomes transparent to every other within society. . . . If thoughts are valid they must be 'yours as much as mine' or they 'are nothing.'"[25] The focus on human experience beyond the body, therefore, made it possible to argue for an aesthetics that could be more collectively experienced, more democratic, and more widely understood and appreciated.

The relationships between subjects and objects are further complicated by other theories as well. We will touch on only two of these: interpellation and projection. While they both argue for a certain dynamic between the subject and the object, the directions of movement are opposite to one another. In interpellation, the object calls to the subject. This is evident in work that invites the subject to attend to it in certain ways, such as through recognition of the mathematics of the cosmos or the principles of nature or even through movement, as in the Werkbund Administration Building and in Le Corbusier's architecture. Whether by means of an invitation to move or to see in certain ways, architecture is designed to "orient" the subject.

Louis Althusser called this "interpellation" or "hailing": "Ideology 'acts' or 'functions' in such a way that it 'recruits subjects among the individuals . . . or 'transforms' the individuals into subjects . . . by the very precise operation which I have called interpellation or hailing, and which can be imagined along the lines of the most commonplace everyday police (or other) hailing: 'Hey, you there!'"[26] We can say the same thing about architecture, as well.

In addition to interpellation, the movement between subjects and objects is activated in reverse by "projection": subjects "project" some aspect of themselves into the space they are viewing or into which they are moving. The concept of projection is generally associated with psychoanalytic theory. It is understood as the tendency to project unconsciously one's own sentiments, emotions, or needs onto and/or into others. The original definition, however, has been expanded to include several techniques that test for personality characteristics; these techniques, such as the Rorschach inkblot test, are designed with the assumption that personality characteristics are revealed in responses to images and questionnaires. Even color is considered a projected experience of visual perception in "eccentric projection": "[v]isual sense data are habitually projected: the pink is seen as on the rose petal, not as on the retina."[27] Certain psychoanalysts consider projective identification an important aspect of psychological health; it is "a mental mechanism whereby the self experiences the unconscious phantasy of translocating itself, or aspects of itself, into an object for exploratory or defensive purposes."[28] While Kant argued that subjects projected their ideas on their sensate experience of the world, others have proposed that we project other aspects of ourselves—our bodies, emotions, and desires, for example. We try to map ourselves onto/into the world.

The idea of projection was evident in aesthetic theories at the turn of the twentieth century, perhaps most clearly in Theodor Lipps's theory of empathy. As Rudolph Arnheim described it,

> [Lipps's] theory of "empathy" was designed to explain why we find expression even in inanimate objects, such as the columns of a temple. . . . When I look at the columns I know from past experience the kind of mechanical pressure and counterpressure that occurs in them. Equally from past experience, I know how I should feel myself if I were in the place of the columns and if those physical forces acted upon and within my own body. I project my own kinesthetic feelings onto the columns. Furthermore, the pressures and pulls called up from the stores of memory by the sight tend also to provoke responses in other areas of the mind. "When I project my strivings and forces into nature I do so also as to the way my strivings and forces make me feel, that is, I project my pride, my courage, my stubbornness, my lightness, my playful assuredness, my tranquil complacence. Only thus my empathy with regard to nature becomes truly aesthetic empathy."[29]

Lipps's theory was based on Wilhelm Worringer's proposals in *Abstrac-tion and Empathy* of the empathetic projection of body experience.[30] Worrin-ger claimed that pleasure or "delight" in aesthetic experience was based on our "feeling" into forms our own body experiences of force, pressure, and stress. John Ruskin expressed a similar concept when he specifically reject-ed iron as a legitimate element in architecture precisely because it made him "feel" uncomfortable as his eye had been trained in the proportions estab-lished through heavy masonry construction.[31] More recently, Elaine Scarry presented an argument in which the body is projected into a work in three different ways. The first describes the phenomenon of projection in terms of "the contiguous relationship of the body to an object" (the spine to the chair or the skin to the bandage/clothing/etc.); the second concerns the identification of "bodily capacities and needs" in an object (photographs, film, tape recordings, and photocopies, for example, are evidence and exten-sion of memory); and the third is used to deprive "the external world of the privilege of being inanimate . . . [which] is almost to say (but is not to say) that the external world is made animate" (kicking a door in anger).[32] In each of these cases, empathy introduced the dynamic, sensible, and lived expe-riences of the body and the projection of the mind or the spirit as sources of aesthetic experience.

Theories of projection and interpellation depend on vision for their ef-fectiveness. This suggests that the relationships between the body and the eye, between empathy and signs, between reading, moving, and feeling, cannot be addressed adequately if we conceive of them as independent ex-periences.[33] In addition, visual and bodily "orientations" and invitations to move suggest the power of architecture to shape what we see and how we see and move in space and time. They also help to clarify what Derrida meant when he claimed that architecture "constructs and instructs" us.

The question of the construction of the subject, however, goes beyond the eye and the body. It can include the ways we think. According to Mark Wigley, architecture has been used often in philosophy as a metaphor. He argues that Heidegger had examined "the way in which philosophy de-scribes itself as architecture" and concluded that, for Heidegger, "the laying of the foundation is the 'projection of the intrinsic possibilities of metaphys-ics' through an interrogation of the condition of the ground."[34] In this con-text, the value of architecture depends on its presence, which is evident in the ways that philosophy employs architectural terms, such as "foundation," "structure," and "ground." When broadly conceived, these terms are used in philosophical arguments to invite experiences that philosophy lacks as a means of proof. Derrida, Wigley, Eisenman, and Tschumi have all comment-ed on the extensive use of architectural metaphors in philosophy and have concluded that such use is dependent on the spatializations and the experience of presence that architecture makes possible. For example, Derrida writes:

> As soon as we speak . . . we are caught in what traditionally are called spatial metaphors, architectural metaphors. Philosophy is full of them: foundations, systems, architectonics, which in philosophy means the art of systems, but even in more everyday language the spatial metaphors are irreducible, unavoidable and anything but accidental. So the problem of space and of being inscribed through language in space . . . compels you to deal with architecture without being aware that you are. From the beginning I, among others, was interested in the authority of space over or in language and in the necessity of taking this into account, of analyzing what rhetoric is figured in the spatial. And of course I, among others, tried to describe within some major philosophical discourses (Plato, Descartes, Kant, among others) the program hidden in the set of architectural metaphors.[35]

The irreducibility of spatial metaphors in language implies that "the philosopher is an architect, endlessly attempting to produce a grounded structure,"[36] and, more important for architecture, each subject repeats its dependence on specific concepts of space and presence whenever it engages in language and thought.

The unavoidability of architecture, and thus its authority, stems from our desire for the presence that architecture provides: its solidity, weight, permanence, and capacity to protect us.[37] Wigley argues that "[t]he question of metaphysics has always been that of the ground (*grund*) on which things stand even though it has been explicitly formulated in these terms only in the modern period inaugurated by Descartes. Metaphysics is no more than the attempt to locate the ground. Its history is that of a succession of different names (logos, ratio, arche . . . etc.) for the ground. Each of them designates 'Being,' which is understood as presence. Metaphysics is the identification of the ground as 'supporting presence' for an edifice."[38]

Critics like Derrida have argued that architecture "constructs and instructs" us because it forms the basis of memory and imagination. Certainly those who argued for a typology of spaces would agree. Writers such as Bachelard have demonstrated that we remember the houses and landscapes of our childhood and tend to repeat those that we cherish. Clare Cooper Marcus's research suggests that young architects as well as people not trained in architecture tend to repeat their favorite childhood places in their work and avoid those for which they have negative associations.[39] From this we might conclude, as we have for thinking, seeing, and moving, that our imaginations are also at least partly shaped by architecture.

Subject-object correlations and the framework of the familiar and the unfamiliar are complicated by the fact that architects are subjects as well. This raises the issue of autobiography, which we mentioned briefly in the work of Rossi, and signature. Yet Rossi is not alone in using autobiography in his architecture. Etlin pointed out that Wright often visited a special area of the Wisconsin valleys near his home, known as the "Driftless Area," while growing up. Wright was deeply impressed by this unglaciated landscape, and he spent a considerable amount of time wandering in it, often returning to favorite lookout points.[40] Etlin has drawn correspondences between this geography, with its clearings and elevated viewing platforms, and his work. It is possible to discern a similar attention to geography in Le Corbusier's work. The promenade, specifically referred to by Colin Rowe as a "topographic" experience, recalls the climb to the Acropolis, a sequence of movements that is illustrated in *Towards a New Architecture* and is evident in Le Corbusier's villas and maisons of the 1920s. Just as Wright's Wisconsin experiences are reflected in his buildings, the promenade might also suggest some of Le Corbusier's experiences in the Jura mountains where he grew up. We might attribute some of the differences between Wright and Le Corbusier to the different landscapes they experienced in their youth, and the kinds of bodies, visual interests, and imaginal possibilities that they associated with them.

In Rossi's work, the idea of autobiography is evident in the parallels he drew between his objects and his personal struggles to become a collective, objective observer. Venturi stated his own personal preferences clearly in the opening paragraph of *Complexity and Contradiction*.[41] The personal struggles that Rossi described and the preferences that Venturi declared are reflected in their work. These more personal dimensions to an architect's work, coupled with their equivalents in the early part of the century, suggest a greater degree of autobiography in architecture than Western culture has been interested in recognizing.

Questions concerning autobiography and subjectivity were a significant part of twentieth-century architectural discourse. They emerged in the early phases of modernism in the critique of self-expression as a form of projection, a concern that later would play a role in Rossi's attempt to transform himself into an objective, scientific, and collective subject. More recently, the question of autobiography emerged in discussions about the architect's "signature" work and the "power of the author," the "author's" (architect's) power to control or dictate the subject's experience.[42] Yet by the end of the twentieth century, the possibility of self-expression by architects, including Eisenman, was paramount. As Dana Cuff points out:

> For Eisenman, the other, in the sense of actual clients is insignificant in light of his existential project: "How do I prove I'm here?" He answers by digging,

inventing, and building. However, it is against the backdrop of others, "the cultural baggage," societal expectations, that he must act in order to plumb his own depths. . . . [He says,] "I look for my Self in *your* mirror, not in my mirror. That would be narcissism." And when he talks about teaching, he implies that the appropriate human context (teacher, group therapy) allows one to recover one's identity. Thus, for Eisenman, the self is fundamentally the only member of the architect's people that can truly be known.[43]

Eisenman's position concerning the role of the architect is diametrically opposed to the modernist proscription against self-expression and subjectivity. Although arguing against the humanist tradition in architecture at times, Eisenman seems to continue it, if Hays's description is correct: "In humanist thought the role of the subject vis-à-vis the object has been that of an originating agent of meaning, unique, centralized, and authoritative. The individual subject enters the dialectic with the world as its source, as the intending manipulator of the object and the conscious originator of meanings and actions."[44] Eisenman was not alone in struggling with questions concerning the power of the author (the architect) over the reader (the addressee of architecture) at the end of the twentieth century.

The idea of autobiography directly relates to the question of signature work, that is, work that can be identified as the work of a particular architect. Architecture bears the "signature" of its architects and can be directly linked to them. Sharing some ideas of Benjamin and Rossi about the conditioning of the subject as well as concerns about commonplace architecture, Frank Gehry took up the issue of signature in the early 1990s. Echoing both Rossi's and Benjamin's arguments, Gehry claimed that "my singularity, my signature, has been conditioned by everything around me. It's intrinsic with all of my values and the values of my time."[45] Nonetheless, it is his signature that he cannot escape. Gehry reinforced the point raised by Eisenman by claiming that "I think that's the weakness of most architecture, that there's so much stuff you can hide behind that you never get to the 'moment of truth.' You're never forced to confront who you are as a person in the equation."[46] In fact, Gehry considered this an important part of a work of architecture, that is, that architects had to invest their work with something of themselves: "What is your move when you've been given all the givens? It's that signature, that oneness, the moment of giving, of a person giving what they have of themselves. It's when you bring your essence to it, your choices. . . . Your own signature is the way you think about it, the way you make your own work, the way you engage the work."[47]

Regardless of their arguments—and Rossi would have argued most vehemently against this—all of the architects in this study have produced works that are widely recognized as their own. No one has been able to copy their work sufficiently to confuse its signature status. Many contemporaries of Wright, some even trained by him, attempted to copy his work but merely copied the style and not the principles that he espoused. He criticized this work severely. Le Corbusier also was copied and some of the same problems resulted; most derivative works were stylistically similar but failed to address the greater complexities that he espoused. A late 1960s revival and extension of Le Corbusier's early work was attempted by the New York Five with varying degrees of success. Although the architectures of Rossi and VSBA suffered similar fates, their signatures are clearly identifiable in their work. The questions of projection, therefore, are not merely those of the person who experiences architecture. They include the architect as well.

The desire for the familiar or the unfamiliar on the part of the architect and the subject is relevant in the study of architecture, especially given the critical responses to architects' works, many of which did not corroborate what the architects had imagined as their subject's experience. For example, early modernist architects found that as modern materials made transparencies possible, the spaces and views that were created challenged the simple boundary that conventional architecture had used to distinguish inside from outside. The use of modern materials to produce new spaces and new experiences disturbed the relationship between inside and outside that was conventionally addressed through windows and doors. In modern architecture, these were often difficult to find, as for example in floor-to-ceiling glass walls with glass doors. Although intended as a liberating experience, the negating of the edges between inside and outside introduced problems of exposure and loss of place for some people. Some of the disturbing and alienating experiences that people reported about modern space were based on these characteristics, returning us to the problem of the separation of the senses (see fig. 89). As Sennett has described it,

> Fully apprehending the outside form within, yet feeling neither cold nor wind nor moisture, is a modern sensation, a modern sensation of protected openness in very big buildings. . . . This model house is a primitive version of the technology that would operate in the skyscraper interior to isolate the interior from the outside, even though everything outside was visible. The combination of visibility and isolation then grew stronger with the development of air conditioning and the thermal glass . . . a half-century later. . . . Though technology has heightened visibility through plate glass, the world made visible through this window has been devalued in its reality. This is true of sensate reality: a man sees from his office window a tree blowing in the wind but cannot hear the wind blowing.[48]

Many critics expressed anxiety and alienation in relation to these conditions. For example, Mark Wigley wrote, "The division between inside and

Figure 89. Edward Hopper, *Room in New York,* 1932. (Courtesy Sheldon Memorial Art Gallery and Sculpture Garden, University of Nebraska, Lincoln)

outside is radically disturbed. . . . [T]he sense of being enclosed, whether by a building or a room, is disrupted. But not by simply removing walls—the closure of form is not simply replaced by the openness of the modern free plan. This is not freedom, liberation, but stress; not release, but greater tension. . . . There are no simple windows, no regular openings puncturing a solid wall; rather the wall is tormented—split and folded. It no longer provides security by dividing the familiar from the unfamiliar, inside from out. The whole condition of enclosure breaks down."[49] Some people missed the framing protection and comfort of windows that premodern architecture typically provided: a sense of human scale; a sheltered place from which to view the exterior; a framed, perhaps even intentionally oriented, experience.[50]

Any questions of correlation between the architect's intentions or projections, the interpellations that the work presents, and the projections of the subject are complicated. It is unclear whether architects succeed in realizing their intentions and whether and how these correspond to those projections made by the subjects of their work. In addition, it is difficult to determine the nature of received meaning. As we have seen, assumptions about the meanings of signs were often misunderstood by critics and the public alike. The experiments by VSBA, for example, were often criticized for focusing on issues that were not considered architectural or for not providing the meanings that the architects claimed. Rafael Moneo wrote:

> We can see the criticism in Venturi's understanding of architectural reality. Here reality is capable of including everything, assuming everything, admitting that communication in the physical world is based more in the support of non-architectural mechanisms than in those that see architecture as a discipline through which the physical world is both transcended and intruded upon. Architecture must be integrated into this process of communication forgetting its specific condition, its own norms; what is interesting is the control of communication, not the intrinsic study of the architectural world, from its internal coherence, the logic of its production; to recover, in a word, the sense that, in today's society, have the forms that specialists look upon as banal.[51]

An intended meaning is often misunderstood. The relationships between sign and interpretations are socially produced, dynamic, and often unpredictable. This problem arose in the criticism of modernism in the 1950s and 1960s and remained a significant part of the discourse of architecture throughout the rest of the century, eventually challenging and undermining most attempts at sign systems. As Ellen Lupton and J. Abbott Miller put it: "By 'post-modernism,' we refer to the culture which absorbed the lessons of the Bauhaus, emptying its forms of their avant-garde aspirations and investing them with new ones. While the visual phrase [yellow triangle] [red square] [blue circle] once embodied the possibility of a universal script, it reappears in contemporary graphics, housewares, packaging, and fashion as a transient sign, bearing such diverse messages as 'originality,' 'technology,' 'design,' 'the basics,' 'modernism,' and even 'post-modernism.'"[52] The certainty of meaning sought in and ascribed to form and space in the modern era seemed less likely in light of the use of politically charged Bauhaus designs for conservative and marketing goals. Ultimately, as Derrida has suggested, meaning is undecidable. Lupton and Miller claimed that, "while many modernist design strategies remain compelling, they must be reopened to account for culture's ability to continually rewrite the meaning of visual form. The language of vision is not self-evident or self-contained, but operates in a broader field of social and linguistic values."[53] Kenneth Frampton raised further concerns about the problem of meaning in architecture, claiming that, "since 1943 the issue of representation—the fundamental problem of meaning in architecture—has recurred again and again, only to be met by repression and denial, or by escapist withdrawal into the supposedly spontaneous and hence popular significance of advertising and media in the consumer economy."[54] His conclusion was that "[t]he practice of architecture now lapses into 'silence.'"[55] This "silence" suggests the possibility that predictable meaning in architecture is impossible.

In the end, the use of the framework of the familiar and the unfamiliar, while not without certain problems, has led us to a first level of inquiry about the architectural subject. There are many other levels or perspectives that need to be brought to bear in the analysis of twentieth-century architecture and many other issues that we should explore if we want the broadest possible idea of the subject. What we have been able to glean from this study, however, suggests an array of subject experiences that have been explored by architects in the twentieth century. These give us an initial sketch of the imagined subject of architecture, a sketch that includes visual and bodily projections and movements in relation to objects that are also inviting and orienting. The subject engages in reading or sensing architecture in various ways, and body memories suggest something deeply embedded that connects our bodies, eyes, and minds, as well as our abilities to think. Architecture can shape our own sense of ourselves, our identity, and thus can construct and instruct us.

The idea of the familiar and the unfamiliar takes on new meaning when we examine the possibilities of architecture's influence on its subjects. In light of the metaphorical nature of architecture, autobiography on the part of architects, and the concepts of interpellation and projection, the point that Derrida put forward concerning the construction and instruction of the subject begins to gain some measure of clarity. Yet the subject is even more complex than we have been able to articulate in this study.

Nonetheless, we can conclude that the architects whose work we have examined here have offered us a wide range of ideas about the subject and, in the process, about the natures and purposes of architecture in relation to it. The imagined subject of architecture is projected and hailed. It is shocked by the new and grounded by the familiar. It is split, complex, imbalanced, moving, multiple, and erased. It is free or dialectical, a single reader and, at least partly, collective in nature. It experiences presence and absence by means of the body and the eye as complex and interdependent modes of experience often correlated with associations and memory. The intentions of the architects we have examined are to balance or integrate it, to ground it, or to shock and defamiliarize it.

The psychological, political, and ethical questions that emerge in this kind of study should reinforce the importance of subject research in architecture. Looking for the subjects that architects imagine in their work, as we have done here, will help us understand the ideas that shape an architect's work. By gaining theoretical perspectives on the works of architects, we are in a better position to speculate about the variety of ideas concerning architecture and its subjects that architects employ.

NOTES

Introduction

1. See, for example, Francis D. K. Ching, *Architecture: Form, Space, and Order* (New York: Van Nostrand Reinhold, 1979).

2. See, for example, Diana Agrest, "Architecture from Without: Body, Logic, and Sex," *Assemblage* 7 (1988): 29–41.

3. Sigfried Giedion, *Space, Time and Architecture: The Growth of a New Tradition,* 4th ed. (Cambridge, Mass.: Harvard University Press, 1974), 13.

4. Ibid., 762–64.

5. K. Michael Hays, *Modernism and the Posthumanist Subject: The Architecture of Hannes Meyer and Ludwig Hilberseimer* (Cambridge, Mass.: MIT Press, 1992), 12.

6. Tschumi is described in the *International Dictionary of Architects and Architecture* as "one of the foremost representatives of Deconstruction" in contemporary architectural theory and practice. *International Dictionary of Architects and Architecture,* ed. Randall J. Van Vynckt (Detroit: St. James Press, 1993), 909.

7. Bernard Tschumi, *Architecture and Disjunction* (Cambridge, Mass.: MIT Press, 1994), 96. I published some preliminary work on Tschumi's subject in "Book Review: *Architecture and Disjunction* and *Event Cities*," *Journal of Architectural Education* 49, no. 2 (Nov. 1995): 132–34.

8. Jacques Derrida, in Mark Wigley, "Jacques Derrida: Invitation to a Discussion," *Columbia Documents of Architecture and Theory: D* 1 (1992): 18.

9. Tschumi, *Architecture and Disjunction,* 237.

10. Ibid., 246.

11. See, for example, Tschumi, *Architecture and Disjunction,* and Peter Eisenman, "En Terror Firma: In Trails of Grotextes," *The Fifth Column 7* 1 (Oct. 1988): 24–27.

12. See Philip Johnson and Mark Wigley, *Deconstructivist Architecture* (New York: Museum of Modern Art, 1988); and Andreas Papadakis, Catherine Cooke, and Andrew Benjamin, eds., *Deconstruction: Omnibus Volume* (New York: Rizzoli, 1989).

13. See Robert Hughes, *The Shock of the New* (New York: Knopf, 1982).

14. Tschumi, *Architecture and Disjunction,* 249.

15. Ibid., 237.

16. Derrida, in Wigley, "Jacques Derrida: Invitation to a Discussion," 26.

17. Wigley, "Jacques Derrida: Invitation to a Discussion," 7–8.

18. Derrida, as quoted in Mark Wigley, "The Translation of Architecture: The Product of Babel," *Architectural Design* 60, nos. 9–10 (1990): 13.

19. Derrida, in Wigley, "Jacques Derrida: Invitation to a Discussion," 24.

20. Grahame Shane, "Contextualism," *Architectural Design* 11 (1976): 676–77. See further discussion of cultural contextualism in chapter 4 of the present work.

21. Ibid., 678. For other discussion of cultural contextualism, see Jean-Louis Sarbib, "Popu-lore Architecture," *L'Architecture d'aujourd'hui* (June 1978): 2–6.

22. Shane, "Contextualism," 676.

23. Rossi's method ultimately prompted international studies of building typologies, a taxonomic attitude shared with neoclassicism. Shane, "Contextualism," 678. See also Martin Filler, "Rossi Secco and Rossi Dolce," *Art in America* (March 1980): 104–6, and Robert Venturi, "Architecture as Shelter, Decoration on It, and Another Plea for a Symbolism of the Ordinary in Architecture," *L'Architecture d'aujourd'hui* (June 1978): 12–19.

24. Shane, "Contextualism," 676.

25. Ibid., 678. For extensive references to the Mediterranean piazza, see Colin Rowe and Fred Koetter, "Collage City," *Architectural Review* 158, no. 942 (August 1975): 66–90, and Robert Venturi, Denise Scott Brown, and Steven Izenour, *Learning from Las Vegas,* rev. ed. (Cambridge, Mass.: MIT Press, 1985).

26. Shane, "Contextualism," 678.

27. For a discussion of the accommodations in VSBA's Oberlin museum addition, see Alan Colquhoun, "Sign and Substance: Reflections on Complexity, Las Vegas, and Oberlin," in his *Essays in Architectural Criticism: Modern Architecture and Historical Change* (Cambridge, Mass.: MIT Press, 1981), 139–51. In his essay, Colquhoun also discusses the evolution of VSBA's theory, from *Complexity* to *Las Vegas.* See also Robert Venturi, "Learning the Right Lessons from the Beaux-Arts," *Architectural Design* 1 (1979): 25, and Sarbib, "Popu-lore Architecture," 4–5. Sarbib provides an excellent overview of Herbert Gans's position concerning "the positive aspects of communities traditionally despised . . . for their 'poor' taste" and his theory of "'cultural pluralism' shared to a large extent by Venturi and Scott-Brown. . . . [The latter] conceives of their role as 'high-culture' architects: she believes in the need for physical parallels to the sociological studies of Gans" (4).

28. Tschumi, *Architecture and Disjunction,* 246.

29. The ideas of the familiar and the unfamiliar were explored throughout the century by such artists as Duchamp and other surrealists and dadaists, as well as by John Cage, Gordon Matta-Clark, Rachel Whiteread, and Lars Lerup.

30. Mikhail Mikhailovich Bakhtin, "Discourse in the Novel," in *Art and Its Significance: An Anthology of Aesthetic Theory,* ed. Stephen David Ross, 2d ed. (Albany: State University of New York Press, 1987), 486–87.

31. *Webster's Encyclopedic Unabridged Dictionary of the English Language* (New York: Portland House, 1989), 1415.

32. Ibid.

33. These investigations included feminism and queer theory, which explored gender and sexual identity, and studies of the "colonial subject," that is, one that is a member of a "colonized" community. The idea of the subject was also of central importance in the criticism of the power of the author in the late 1970s and at the heart of reader-response theory in the 1980s. Recent client-based research and scholarship and other theories concerning identity emerged in studies of race, ethnicity, class, region, nation, and religion.

34. Richard Sennett, *The Conscience of the Eye* (New York: Norton, 1992), 97. Sennett points out that Hannah Arendt suggested this as the basis for what she referred to as "the exile's voyage to citizenship from his or her past"; this entails a "'disappearance of the subject,' which means that each person's 'I,' by a painful and indeed unwilling passage, ought to become less and less important." Ibid., 136.

35. See, for example, Joan Copjec, *Read My Desire: Lacan against the Historicists* (Cambridge, Mass.: MIT Press, 1994). The end of the humanist subject is explored in Hays, *Modernism and the Posthumanist Subject.*

36. Jacques Derrida, "Point de Folie—Maintenant L'architecture," *AA Files* 12 (1986): 65.

37. In order to remain true to the architects I am reviewing, my analysis will remain as close to the "voices" and the "points of view" of the individual authors as possible, as expressed in their writings. At times, as in the work of Giedion and Tschumi, the subjects that are assumed by the authors are clearly stated. At other times, the subjects are less clear and to uncover them I have closely analyzed the architects' texts, extrapolating the language that each used. This process formed the basis for identifying keywords and phrases that authors employed in relation to the subject. I will use the results of such analyses in uncovering the theoretical definitions of the imagined subjects assumed in the texts of the author-architects. These will assist us in better understanding the people that architects imagine for their buildings. This study does not extend its analysis to include the graphic design and composition of the original text as additional evidence of an architect's intentions toward the reader.

38. The distinction between Venturi's work and that of Denise Scott Brown, his business partner and wife, is difficult to establish with certainty. In the "Acknowledgements" in *Complexity and Contradiction in Architecture,* Venturi recognized her for "sharing her insights into architecture and city planning." Robert Venturi, *Complexity and Contradiction in Architecture,* 2d ed. (New York: Museum of Modern Art, 1979), 6. In Scott Brown's "Preface to the Revised Edition" of *Learning from Las Vegas,* she specifically criticized those who failed to acknowledge her contributions to that later book: "Robert Venturi's note on attribution in the first edition, with its request for fairness to his co-authors and co-workers, was virtually ignored by almost all reviewers. Personal pique at the cavalier handling of my contribution and at attribution in general by architects and journalists led me to analyze the social structure of the profession, its domination by upper-class males, and the emphasis its members place upon the architectural star system. The result is an article entitled 'Sexism and the Star System in Architecture'" (xv–xvi). Scott Brown "has been involved with Venturi in the development of architectural theory since the early 1960s" (*Macmillan Encyclopedia of Architects,* 4 vols., ed. Adolf K. Placzek [New York: Free Press, 1982], 4:307), before the publication of *Complexity and Contradiction* (1966), making the differentiation of their individual contributions to the work quite difficult. During the period considered in the present study, Robert Venturi was also in partnership with others, such as William Short (Guild House, Vanna Venturi House) and John Rauch, and published with Steven Izenour, all of whom had some influence on the subjects and objects as well as on the position that we will refer to as that of Venturi Scott Brown and Associates, or VSBA.

39. Each architect is listed in the *International Dictionary of Architects and Architecture* and/or in the *Macmillan Encyclopedia of Architects,* the two most important English-

language reference works on architects and architecture for the general public. Frank Lloyd Wright, Le Corbusier, and Robert Venturi are listed in the *Macmillan Encyclopedia of Architects,* 4:434–48; 2:630–48; and 4:305–8, respectively; and Frank Lloyd Wright, Le Corbusier, Aldo Rossi, and Robert Venturi in the *International Dictionary of Architects and Architecture,* 997–1003, 494–500, 752–53, and 944–46, respectively.

40. Each of the texts is mentioned either in the *Macmillan Encyclopedia of Architects* or in the *International Dictionary of Architects and Architecture* as "important," "seminal," and even a "benchmark" text. This study concentrates on seminal texts as representative of a dominant professional and "popular" culture. I selected these texts because they have been widely published, read, and cited in architectural scholarship, among professionals as well as people outside the discipline. My study is fundamentally concerned with the popular and professional understanding of the intended subject in twentieth-century architecture in the West. This is the same reason that I have used the *International Dictionary of Architects and Architecture* and the *Macmillan Encyclopedia of Architects* as general references.

The *Arts and Humanities Citation Index* (Philadelphia: Institute for Scientific Information, 1975–98) recorded the following number of citations from the period 1975–98 for these texts: Wright's "The Art and Craft of the Machine," "The Sovereignty of the Individual," and "In the Cause of Architecture" (44); Le Corbusier's *Towards a New Architecture* (164); Rossi's *The Architecture of the City* (69); and Venturi's *Complexity and Contradiction* (196). The *Social Sciences Citation Index* recorded the following number of citations from the period 1976–98: *Towards a New Architecture* (25), *The Architecture of the City* (31), and *Complexity and Contradiction* (47). The number of citations of Frank Lloyd Wright's essays is difficult to count because they have been republished in several collections. Two other texts that figure prominently in this study are Aldo Rossi, *A Scientific Autobiography,* trans. Lawrence Venuti (Cambridge, Mass.: MIT Press, 1981), and Venturi, Scott Brown, and Izenour, *Learning from Las Vegas.* The number of citations of these works as reported by the *Arts and Humanities Citation Index* were 19 and 162, respectively, and by the *Social Sciences Citation Index,* 6 and 67, respectively.

41. Frank Lloyd Wright's first architectural text was his Wasmuth portfolio, the *Ausgeführte Bauten und Entwürfe von Frank Lloyd Wright* (Berlin: Wasmuth, 1910). It was reprinted numerous times, including as an introduction to an exhibition of Wright's work at the Palazzo Strozzi in Florence, in 1951; as *Drawings and Plans of Frank Lloyd Wright* (New York: Dover, 1983); and as *Studies and Executed Buildings by Frank Lloyd Wright* (New York: Rizzoli, 1986). Wright's first book was *The Japanese Print,* but it is less helpful for this study than his essays about architecture. Wright's preface to that book has been republished several times under the title "The Sovereignty of the Individual," testifying to its significance for Wright and for those involved in the history and criticism of his work. See Wright, "The Sovereignty of the Individual," in *Frank Lloyd Wright: Writings and Buildings,* ed. Edgar Kaufmann and Ben Raeburn (New York: New American Library, 1974). In order to gain a sufficiently broad perspective of Wright's ideas, I have consulted several other pieces, two of which are important early essays: "The Art and Craft of the Machine" (1901) and "In the Cause of Architecture" (1914). Both have been republished often in various collections of Wright's essays. For example, both appear in Kaufmann and Raeburn, *Frank Lloyd Wright,* 55–73 and 181–96, respectively. "In the Cause of Architecture" was originally published in *Architectural Record* for March 1908 and was so successful that it was followed by other pieces in those pages (1914, 1925). It was republished in a collection of essays from *Architectural Record* entitled *In the Cause of Architecture: Essays by Frank Lloyd Wright for Architectural Record, 1908–1952,* ed. F. Gutheim, (New York: McGraw-Hill, 1975). In the entry on Wright in the *Macmillan Encyclopedia of Architects,* Edgar Kaufmann Jr. declared that "The Art and Craft of the Machine" was "one of Wright's best statements" and the Wasmuth portfolio was "acclaimed" (4:437–38). These early texts will form the basis of our study of the architecture that Wright produced during the same period.

42. Le Corbusier's *Towards a New Architecture,* considered by some to be "the single most influential text" on architecture in the twentieth century, was largely a compilation of essays and propaganda pieces that he had published in the late 1910s in the avant-garde magazine *L'Esprit nouveau. International Dictionary of Architects and Architecture,* 499. *Towards a New Architecture* has become the exemplar against which many subsequent publications have been measured.

43. Aldo Rossi's *L'architettura della città* was first published in 1966 and republished in several languages and many editions. See, for example, Rossi, *The Architecture of the City,* trans. Diane Ghirardo (Cambridge, Mass.: MIT Press, 1991). It is regarded, especially in Europe, as one of the most important architectural treatises in the post–World War II era. "There have been only a handful of architects whose theoretical writings have significantly affected the evolution of architecture since World War II. Among these is Aldo Rossi, whose 1966 treatise *L'architettura della città [The Architecture of the City]* clearly countered the tenets of the Modern Movement. . . . Just as Robert Venturi's *Complexity and Contradiction in Architecture* is a benchmark in the development of postmodernism in architecture in the United States, Rossi's *L'architettura . . .* indicates a divergent direction for contemporary architecture. . . . Rossi has affected the direction of architecture and design for much of the younger generation." *International Dictionary of Architects and Architecture,* 752. Although *A Scientific Autobiography* is a significant text in its own right, I am using it here primarily to gain access to the assumptions about the subject largely implicit in *The Architecture of the City.*

44. Venturi's *Complexity and Contradiction* was considered by some critics as equal in importance to Le Corbusier's *Towards a New Architecture.* In his introduction to the second edition of Venturi's publication, Vincent Scully stated that he considered Le Corbusier's text the most important writing on twentieth-century architecture before the publication of Venturi's book, which became a benchmark because it exposed the weaknesses of the modern movement at a time when the movement had lost some of its momentum. Vincent Scully, "Introduction," in Venturi, *Complexity and Contradiction,* 9. Some critics even suggested that the book itself "was a critical factor in its [the modern movement's] decline." *International Dictionary of Architects and Architecture,* 945. Together with *Learning from Las Vegas, Complexity and Contradiction* "helped to redefine the territory of architecture by emphasizing issues such as history, language, form, symbolism, and the dialectics of high and popular art. . . . [The two books are] often referred to as marking the 'watershed' that separates the modernist past from the 'absolutely delightful' postmodernist future." Philip C. Johnson, as quoted in *Macmillan Encyclopedia of Architects,* 4:305. In 1987, Michael J. Crosbie stated that "Robert Venturi's *Complexity and Contradiction in Architecture* remains a landmark in the history of architecture: a book . . . that appears to have changed the course of American architecture." Michael J. Crosbie, "Shaping Our Thinking—and Buildings," *Architecture: AIA Journal* (Dec. 87): 147–49.

Chapter 1: Frank Lloyd Wright

1. In using the term "Machine," Wright meant not only machines in the literal sense, but also the consequences of machines, such as new power, new materials, new ways of construction, and the new possibilities that machines seemed to promise. He used the term to stand in for any or all of these issues, depending on the context.

2. Frank Lloyd Wright, "The Art and Craft of the Machine (1901)," in Bruce Brooks Pfeiffer, ed., *Frank Lloyd Wright Collected Writings,* 5 vols. (New York: Rizzoli, 1992), 1:63.

3. Don Gifford, "Introduction," in *The Literature of Architecture: The Evolution of Architectural Theory and Practice in Nineteenth-Century America,* ed. Don Gifford (New York: Dutton, 1966), 23–24.

4. Ibid.

5. William J. R. Curtis, *Modern Architecture since 1900,* 2d ed. (Englewood Cliffs: Prentice-Hall, 1987), 56.

6. John Ruskin, *The Seven Lamps of Architecture* (New York: Farrar, Straus and Giroux, 1974), 43–44.

7. Ibid.

8. Wright, "The Art and Craft of the Machine," 64.

9. Wright and Sullivan were not alone in advocating these ideas. According to Don Gifford, "[t]he ideal of an 'organic' architecture in which 'form follows function' seems to have been approached simultaneously by a number of individuals, working from a variety of different points of view and using at times deceptively similar vocabularies. It seems to have been an ideal that was 'in the air.'" Gifford, *The Literature of Architecture,* 17. In looking back to the nineteenth century, however, the person that we most associate with these concepts is Louis H. Sullivan. Sullivan's definition of the "organic," like his other ideas, is complex. As Gifford explains: "the word 'organic' suggests a variety of possibilities: that an architectural form should be like a natural organism, that the interrelation of parts to each other and to the whole should be 'natural,' that the relation of a building to its occupants and their pursuits should be natural and plastic, that the relation of a building to its site and to the natural world should be in organic continuum. All this variety crops up in nineteenth-century speculation, and has hardly been clarified into more than a suggestive ideal, even by Frank Lloyd Wright, its great twentieth-century exponent." In addition, Gifford says, "The ideal of organic form is further complicated when it is interrelated with ideals of fitness and utility: that a building's forms should fit and not disguise the uses for which the building is intended. This complication is compounded by the wide-ranging definitions of 'use,' and consequently of 'fitness.' 'Use' can be defined in terms of crass utility; it can also be defined, following Emerson's suggestion, in terms of the aesthetic, moral, and intellectual usefulness of beauty." Ibid., 20. William Morris used the term in a similar way. According to Philip Henderson, "Morris states once more that if we are ever to have architecture at all, we must take up the thread of living tradition from where the medieval builders left it, 'because that Gothic Architecture is the most completely organic form of the Art which the world has seen.'" Philip Henderson, *William Morris: His Life, Work, and Friends* (London: Thames and Hudson, 1967), 208.

10. Philip Fisher, "Democratic Social Space: Whitman, Melville, and the Promise of American Transparency," *Representations* 24 (Fall 1988): 75–76.

11. Ibid., 64–65.

12. Ibid., 67.

13. According to Fisher, this applies to the family as well: "Jefferson's picture of America as a nation of independent family farms, self-sufficient, not so large that they could not be worked by family members alone, stable, neither increasing nor decreasing in size or wealth, contented and independent: this was one of the first and most enduring images of democratic social space. All farms would be very similar because each would provide completely for the needs of the family. The larger society might be made up of an unlimited number of such households. Such farms would also be isomorphic. A family could move from one such farm in Virginia to another in Nebraska and reduplicate their way of life, carry it on without resistance other than from changes in landscape and climate." As Fisher points out, "The modern American suburb is another such Cartesian, democratic social space. Everywhere across the varied geography and climate the suburbs are comfortably the same, equipped with the same schools and parks for children; the same shopping centers with the same stores selling Levi's, Tide, and power lawn mowers." Fisher, "Democratic Social Space," 65.

14. Ibid., 64 (first quote), 65 (second quote).

15. Ibid., 68–69.

16. Lionel Trilling, *The Experience of Literature: A Reader with Commentaries* (New York: Doubleday, 1967), 907.

17. Ibid., 909.

18. Wright, "The Sovereignty of the Individual," 92–93.

19. Ibid.

20. Ibid.

21. Louis H. Sullivan, *Kindergarten Chats and Other Essays* (New York: Dover, 1979), 207-8.

22. Ibid., 44.

23. Ibid., 43-44.

24. Frank Lloyd Wright, "In the Cause of Architecture: The Third Dimension," in Pfeiffer, *Frank Lloyd Wright Collected Writings,* 1:212.

25. Henry David Thoreau, *Walden* (New York: Macmillan, 1962), 44-45.

26. Sullivan, "XIX. Responsibility: The Public," *Kindergarten Chats,* 63-66. Many of the American romantics proposed the same concepts of individuality and the democratic life that Sullivan described. Henry David Thoreau's *Walden,* for example, was "a Jeffersonian experiment to spell out the unit of self-sufficient life. . . . It is the repeatable pattern for a nation of self-sufficient poet/farmers. An entire earth could be carpeted from end to end with reduplications of Thoreau's experiment." Fisher, "Democratic Social Space," 65.

27. Wright, "The Sovereignty of the Individual," 92-93. Like many others in nineteenth-century Western culture, Wright uses the term "man" to represent all human beings, including women. An extended study of Wright's subject would examine the gender-specific evidence in his language and his architecture as well. In addition, more research needs to be done on the houses he did for clients if we are to understand fully the subtle ways that he attempted to use architecture as a medium for individual portraiture.

28. Russell Ellis, "Wright's Written People," in *Architects' People,* ed. Russell Ellis and Dana Cuff (New York: Oxford University Press, 1989), 48.

29. Jack Quinan, "Frank Lloyd Wright, Darwin D. Martin, and the Creation of the Martin House," *Prairie House Journal* (April 1987): 5-6.

30. Ibid.

31. Ibid., 6.

32. Ibid., 8.

33. Ibid., 9-11.

34. Wright, "The Art and Craft of the Machine," 65-66.

35. Ibid., 60.

36. Ibid., 67.

37. Norberg-Schulz, *Meaning in Western Architecture,* 182-83.

38. Richard Etlin, *Frank Lloyd Wright and Le Corbusier: The Romantic Legacy* (New York: Manchester University Press, 1994), 34-35.

39. The visual argument is evident in Jay Appleton's theory of prospect-and-refuge, which Grant Hildebrand applies to Wright's work. Grant Hildebrand, *Origins of Architectural Pleasure* (Berkeley: University of California Press, 1999), 21-49. But Hildebrand also discusses the route traveled by someone from the outside to the center of a Wright house, the hearth; see Grant Hildebrand, *The Wright Space: Pattern and Meaning in Frank Lloyd Wright's Houses* (Seattle: University of Washington Press, 1991), 28-47.

40. Etlin, *Frank Lloyd Wright and Le Corbusier,* 42, 47.

41. Ibid., 39.

42. Ibid., 42, 47.

43. Ibid. In a number of Wright's later works, such as the Affleck House in Bloomfield Hills, Michigan, the curve of the driveway, like a spiral, curls into the house as center. En route, views of the building are presented that, together, give us an "idea" about the architecture.

44. Wright, "The Sovereignty of the Individual," 105-6.

45. Wright, "In the Cause of Architecture," 93.

46. Ibid., 212.

47. Wright, "The Sovereignty of the Individual," 105.

Chapter 2: Le Corbusier

1. Le Corbusier, *Towards a New Architecture,* trans. Frederick Etchells (New York: Dover Publications, 1986), 3. We should note, as we have in Wright's use of the term "man," Le Corbusier's exclusive use of male pronouns. This implies his Enlightenment tendencies, in which "man" is conceived as a term that meant all human beings, regardless of gender.

2. Ibid., 288.

3. Ibid.

4. Ibid., 138.

5. Frederick Etchells, "Introduction," in Le Corbusier, *Towards a New Architecture,* vi.

6. Ibid.

7. Le Corbusier, *Towards a New Architecture,* 101.

8. Ibid., 271.

9. Ibid., 22–23, 277.

10. Ibid., 278–79.

11. Ibid., 288.

12. Le Corbusier, "Towards a New Architecture: Guiding Principles (1920)," in *Programs and Manifestoes on Twentieth-Century Architecture,* ed. Ulrich Conrads (Cambridge, Mass.: MIT Press, 1993), 62.

13. Françoise Choay, *Le Corbusier* (New York: Braziller, 1960), 19–21.

14. Ibid., 19.

15. This split repeats a similar pattern of thought evident in the split of his objects and with the same dialectical synthesis intended. Colin Rowe, *The Mathematics of the Ideal Villa and Other Essays* (Cambridge, Mass.: MIT Press, 1985), 42. Le Corbusier uses an argument similar to that of Adolf Loos. See Adolf Loos, "Ornament and Crime," in Ludwig Münz and Gustav Künstler, *Adolf Loos: Pioneer of Modern Architecture* (New York: Praeger, 1966), 226–31.

16. Le Corbusier, *Towards a New Architecture,* 212.

17. Ibid., 142–43.

18. Rowe, *The Mathematics of the Ideal Villa,* 196.

19. Le Corbusier, *Towards a New Architecture,* 139.

20. Ibid., 220.

21. Ibid., 47.

22. Ibid., 16.

23. Rowe, *The Mathematics of the Ideal Villa,* 42. Le Corbusier was "preoccupied with the Golden Section and the supposed constant laws of perception. . . . [Therefore, his architecture was] given a geometrically disciplined visual form." Curtis, *Modern Architecture,* 107.

24. Le Corbusier, *Towards a New Architecture,* 143.

25. Choay, *Le Corbusier,* 19–21. The promenade also introduced time into Le Corbusier's work. The simplest version is the timeline of movement. A more complex space-time relationship emerges, however, when elements in one part of the architecture remind us of others elsewhere in it. These experiences generate a simultaneity, an experience of déjà vu. Thus, the promenade demonstrated an architecture that addressed issues that had become of central importance in physics. Sigfried Giedion argued that architecture must also address the new world of space-time. See Giedion, *Space, Time and Architecture.*

26. Le Corbusier, *Towards a New Architecture,* 71–72.

27. Choay, *Le Corbusier,* 19–21.

28. See Le Corbusier, *Modulor I and II,* trans. Peter De Francia and Anna Bostock (Cambridge, Mass.: Harvard University Press, 1980). Figure 29 in the present book is based on Leonardo's "Vitruvian man."

29. The relationship of the promenade to the tradition of the *marché* taught at the École des Beaux-Arts is important. The marché was a sequence of rooms and experiences designed to achieve the effects appropriate to the functional type under con-

sideration. A museum, for example, would include a series of preliminary experiences designed to eliminate or reduce the cares and concerns of the "real" world as a way of preparing the visitor for the qualities of the art experience for which the museum, as an institutional type, was constructed. The idea that architecture could be designed to shape the emotional life of the subject was already widely assumed in the nineteenth century. But Le Corbusier criticized the specific way in which Beaux-Arts training led designers to focus on such superficialities as "snow-flake" patterns in plans for decorative purposes, rather than placing their design emphasis on functional spatial arrangements and human experience.

30. Le Corbusier, as quoted in Etlin, *Frank Lloyd Wright and Le Corbusier,* 112–13.

31. Ibid., 114.

32. Le Corbusier, as quoted in Beatriz Colomina, *Privacy and Publicity: Modern Architecture as Mass Media* (Cambridge, Mass.: MIT Press, 1994), 6.

33. Colomina, *Privacy and Publicity,* 6.

34. Kenneth Frampton, "Editor's Introduction," *Oppositions* 15/16 (Winter/Spring 1979): 5–7.

35. This was the basic dialectical practice in Le Corbusier's work throughout his life, although his late work replaced machine forms with local and culturally contextual symbolism, such as references to the bull, a sacred animal, in some of his projects in India. Etlin also mentions the correspondences between the Maison Cook entry and the Farman Goliath airplane. Etlin, *Frank Lloyd Wright and Le Corbusier,* 195–96.

36. By means of the promenade, the viewer could also gain a measure of a similar economy of means reflected in both of the historical conditions that he abstracted. Choay, *Le Corbusier,* 19–21. Some of the machine forms that Le Corbusier used are also related to the body. They are used in bathrooms and as elements of circulation. If we couple this interpretation of his forms with the phenomenal spatial matrix and the harmonies and centralizing tendencies established by the pilotis, we might also grasp how his architecture could be understood as a classic, Cartesian dialectic between the mind and the body. It is the constant repetition of the dialectic in his work at many and different levels that caused Colin Rowe to claim that Le Corbusier was the greatest dialectician of his time. Rowe, *Mathematics of the Ideal Villa,* 194.

37. Rowe, *Mathematics of the Ideal Villa,* 186.

38. Etlin, *Frank Lloyd Wright and Le Corbusier,* 119–20.

39. Ibid., 123.

40. Le Corbusier, *Towards a New Architecture,* 72.

41. Ibid., 217.

42. Ibid., 212.

43. Ibid., 129.

44. Ibid. Etlin argues that Le Corbusier's artistic achievements, which were milestones of twentieth-century culture, were guided by a nineteenth-century progressive vision— a historicist (cultural relativist), eclectic, and picturesque, that is, Romantic view. Ibid. His substantive discussion of the promenade can be found on pages 112–19. Thus, from one perspective, the promenade was a late development of the picturesque tradition.

45. Etlin, *Frank Lloyd Wright and Le Corbusier,* 198. As Kurt Forster has observed about the Maison La Roche–Jeanneret, the promenade evolved over time to include the automobile: "Entrance into the [cul-de-sac] . . . is also conceptual initiation into the sphere of Le Corbusier's architectural definition of space." Kurt W. Forster, "Antiquity and Modernity in the La Roche–Jeanneret Houses of 1923," *Oppositions* 15/16 (Winter/Spring 1979): 139. As some have argued, the promenade in the Villa Savoye should include the drive from Paris and the return. The automobile left its mark in the driveway that creates the first-floor curve and in the heart of the building itself: the ramp inserted the latent presence of the automobile into the house and changed the character of domestic space by inserting elements that seemed no longer reserved exclusively for humans. Etlin, *Frank Lloyd Wright and Le Corbusier,* 115.

46. Le Corbusier, *Towards a New Architecture,* 212.

47. Ibid., 208.

48. Ibid., 1.

49. Ibid., 148. Le Corbusier's clients were generally bourgeois, either aesthetes of the upper bourgeoisie or fashionable speculators. Frampton, "Editor's Introduction," 9.

50. Le Corbusier, *Towards a New Architecture,* 278.

51. Choay, *Le Corbusier,* 19–21.

52. Ibid. One of the sections of *Towards a New Architecture* is directed to those with "Eyes Which Do Not See." Le Corbusier, *Towards a New Architecture,* 85–148.

53. Choay, *Le Corbusier,* 14.

54. Frampton, "Editor's Introduction," 2.

55. Charles Jencks, *Le Corbusier and the Tragic View of Architecture* (Cambridge, Mass.: Harvard University Press, 1974), 12.

56. Ibid., 13.

57. Choay, *Le Corbusier,* 19.

58. Ibid., 5.

59. Frampton, "Editor's Introduction," 3, 7. Frampton calls Le Corbusier "messianic" and discusses his Albigensian and Manichaean propensities. Ibid., 11.

60. Ibid., 7.

61. Jencks, *Le Corbusier and the Tragic View,* 12.

Chapter 3: Aldo Rossi

1. Rossi, *A Scientific Autobiography,* 22.

2. Ibid., 2.

3. Ibid., 80.

4. Rossi, *The Architecture of the City,* 41.

5. Rossi, *A Scientific Autobiography,* 22.

6. Rossi, *The Architecture of the City,* 40.

7. Ibid., 41 (first quote), 88 (second quote); Rossi, *A Scientific Autobiography,* 15 (third quote). Rossi's interest in Nietzsche is significant in this regard. Nietzsche's comment that the primary goal of a philosopher was to be "timeless" might be examined in relation to Rossi's desire to "make architecture and furniture which transcend time and function." Ibid., 74.

8. Rossi, *A Scientific Autobiography,* 41. Giedion imagined that subjects and objects related in important ways, even to the extent that the one mirrored the other. K. Michael Hays argued that "the rift involved a split in subjective or psychological terms between thought and feeling, and in objective, architectural terms between form and structure, expression and construction, art and industrial production." Hays, *Modernism and the Posthumanist Subject,* 15.

Rossi attributes positive value to the "loss of identity" at the Mosque of Bursa. Rossi, *A Scientific Autobiography,* 52. However, it is important to consider what Rossi might have meant by the phrase. In some instances he is ambiguous: "Identity is something unique, typical, but it is also a choice." Ibid., 16. In other statements he seems to be clearer: "Memory and specificity as characteristics enabling the recognition of the self and of what is foreign to it seem to me the clearest conditions and explanations of reality. Specificity can not exist without memory, nor can memory that does not emanate from a specific moment: only the union of the two permits the awareness of one's own individuality and its opposite (of *self* and *non-self*)." Ibid., 62.

9. Rossi, *A Scientific Autobiography,* 19. Memories of his "bourgeois" childhood are a frequent topic of Rossi's second major English-language publication, *A Scientific Autobiography:* "In my bourgeois childhood, I felt excluded by these houses [the 'house of Seville' and 'the houses of old Milan'], and I entered the courtyards with curiosity and fear." Ibid., 19. His struggle with a bourgeois childhood is similar to that of Walter Benjamin, whom Rossi mentions in his work. For a discussion of Benjamin's struggle,

see Susan Buck-Morss, *The Dialectics of Seeing: Walter Benjamin and the Arcades Project* (Cambridge, Mass.: MIT Press, 1991).

10. Rossi, *A Scientific Autobiography*, 23.

11. Ibid., 15.

12. Ibid., 53.

13. Ibid., 83.

14. Ibid., 43.

15. Ibid.

16. Peter Eisenman, "Editor's Introduction: The Houses of Memory, The Texts of Analogy," in *The Architecture of the City;* see, for example, pp. 4, 5, 8, 10.

17. Rossi reports this in Aldo Rossi, "An Analogical Architecture," *Architecture and Urbanism* 56 (May 1976): 74. "Purism" was the name of the style of an art group that included Le Corbusier and Ozenfant for a few years in the late 1910s and early 1920s. The use of the term in relation to Rossi's work must be examined in relation to their work.

18. Rossi himself talked about these years as if they were a period in his work. Aldo Rossi, "Thoughts about My Recent Work," *Architecture and Urbanism* 56 (May 1976): 83.

19. As quoted in *Aldo Rossi: Buildings and Projects,* ed. Peter Arnell and Ted Bickford (New York: Rizzoli, 1985), 126.

20. See, for example, Eisenman, "Editor's Introduction."

21. In the "Introduction" to *Aldo Rossi: Selected Writings and Projects,* for example, Sheila O'Donnell juxtaposes de Chirico's *The Mystery and Melancholy of a Street* with a photograph of the Gallaratese housing project. Sheila O'Donnell, "Introduction," in *Aldo Rossi: Selected Writings and Projects,* ed. John O'Regan, Paul Keogh, Sheila O'Donnell, and Shane O'Toole (Dublin: Gandon Editions, 1983), 11. Martin Filler also discusses this correspondence in his article "Rossi Secco and Rossi Dolce," *Art in America* (March 1980): 102–4.

22. Rafael Moneo, "Aldo Rossi: The Idea of Architecture and the Modena Cemetery," trans. Angela Giral, *Oppositions* (Summer 1976): 18.

23. Rossi, *A Scientific Autobiography*, 15.

24. Vincent Scully, "Postscript," in Rossi, *A Scientific Autobiography*, 116.

25. Jean La Marche, "In and Out of Type," in *Ordering Space: Types in Architecture and Design,* ed. Karen A. Franck and Lynda H. Schneekloth (New York: Van Nostrand Reinhold, 1994), 217. I thank John Knesl for this idea. This is a radically different dialectical architecture than that of Le Corbusier. See Rowe, "La Tourette," in *The Mathematics of the Ideal Villa.*

26. Alan Colquhoun, "Rational Architecture," *Architectural Design* 45, no. 6 (1975): 366.

27. Scully, "Postscript," 111.

28. Rossi, *The Architecture of the City,* 13.

29. Rossi, *A Scientific Autobiography,* 52.

30. Ibid., 80.

31. Ibid., 19.

32. Rossi, *The Architecture of the City,* 107.

33. Ibid., 106–7.

34. Eisenman, "Editor's Introduction," 6 (first quote), 8 (second quote), 9 (third quote).

35. Rossi, *A Scientific Autobiography,* 78.

36. Ibid., 53.

37. Rossi, *The Architecture of the City,* 18.

38. Ibid., 130.

39. Rossi, *A Scientific Autobiography,* 62. Some critics note a melancholic quality to Rossi's work. See Diane Ghirardo, "Introduction: The Theater of Shadows," in *Aldo Rossi: 1981–1991,* ed. Morris Adjmi (New York: Princeton Architectural Press, 1991), 15.

40. Rossi, "Thoughts about My Recent Work," 83.

41. Rossi, "An Analogical Architecture," 74.

42. Ibid., 75.

43. Eisenman, "Editor's Introduction," 11.

Chapter 4: Venturi Scott Brown and Associates

1. Venturi, *Complexity and Contradiction,* 16.

2. Ibid.

3. As noted earlier, Denise Scott Brown reminded readers of this request and chided people who had not honored it. See note 36 of the Introduction, above.

4. Venturi, *Complexity and Contradiction,* 88. Venturi cites others, such as Josef Albers, who assumed similar complexity. Ibid., 16.

5. Ibid., 43.

6. This characterization of VSBA's subject was acceptable to Robert Venturi. Telephone interview by author, August 10, 1995.

7. Venturi, Brown, and Izenour, *Learning from Las Vegas,* 128. Alan Colquhoun considered this "a passage so crucial that it is worth quoting in full." He believed that *Learning from Las Vegas* dealt "a death blow to *Complexity and Contradiction,* whose argument it both condenses and parodies." Colquhoun, *Essays in Architectural Criticism,* 142.

8. Venturi, *Complexity and Contradiction,* 82. The term is used in contemporary practice to indicate the graphic code used in working drawings to fill the space between the outer and inner surfaces of walls. The code indicates the type of material or construction used to fabricate the wall.

9. Ibid., 78. Vincent Scully suggests that Venturi might have created his own kind of layering, one not derived from Louis Kahn. See Vincent Scully, "Everybody Needs Everything," in *Mother's House: The Evolution of Vanna Venturi's House in Chestnut Hill,* ed. Frederic Schwartz (New York: Rizzoli, 1992), 39–57.

10. *International Dictionary of Architects and Architecture,* 946.

11. Venturi, *Complexity and Contradiction,* 82. As understood by VSBA, poché might be compared to the coexistence of both the transparencies and machine forms that are the basis of the dialectic in Le Corbusier's work to suggest a retreat from abstraction in the firm's work. See Etlin, *Frank Lloyd Wright and Le Corbusier,* 119–20.

12. Venturi, *Complexity and Contradiction,* 82.

13. VSBA criticized the limited palette of thin planes in modern architecture in which plastic qualities were very limited. As a result of the interest in the efficient and economic use of materials and construction techniques—except for certain significant examples, such as Le Corbusier, with whom we might compare VSBA and Kahn regarding an interest in poché—the "modernist" wall was understood as a plane. A necessary consequence of this concept is that the wall could not take on any forms outside those made possible by the efficient use of materials and construction practices. In his early criticism of modernist practices, Venturi quoted Aldo van Eyck, who disparaged "the contemporary concept (call it sickness) of spatial continuity and the tendency to erase every articulation between spaces, i.e., between outside and inside, between one space and another (between one reality and another)." Aldo van Eyck, as quoted in Venturi, *Complexity and Contradiction,* 82.

14. The house has been accorded almost iconic status in twentieth-century architecture by critics and historians. It has been compared to Le Corbusier's Villa Savoye with respect to its impact on architecture and to Wright's Oak Park home and certain shingle style houses in regard to general imagery and certain spatial and material conditions.

15. Venturi's *Complexity and Contradiction* and his mother's house were under development at the same time.

16. Schwartz, *Mother's House,* 31. The pattern of distorted symmetry is also repeated in other VSBA works, in which it began at the center as a symmetrical plan, the order of which eroded toward the edges. This, according to VSBA, was a demonstration of the accommodation of the building to its internal functional requirements as

well as to its site and general context. As noted briefly in the Introduction, Grahame Shane suggested that this practice was a common one in "the American school of contextualism" at Cornell University. He pointed to the work of Rowe and Slutzky to demonstrate strategies similar to those of VSBA, and he argued that both showed a "deference towards the existing situation and pragmatic manipulations of the periphery." Shane, "Contextualism," 678.

17. Scully, "Everybody Needs Everything," 53.

18. Stanislaus von Moos, "A Postscript on History, 'Architecture Parlante' and Populism," *Venturi, Rauch and Scott Brown* (Dec. 1981): 202.

19. Robert Venturi, "Residence in Chestnut Hill," in Schwartz, *Mother's House,* 33.

20. Venturi, *Complexity and Contradiction,* 16.

21. VSBA uses the term a total of eleven times in *Complexity and Contradiction* and *Learning from Las Vegas.*

22. Venturi, Scott Brown, and Izenour, *Learning from Las Vegas,* 91.

23. Venturi, *Complexity and Contradiction,* 43.

24. Ibid., 61.

25. Wordsworth, as quoted in Venturi, *Complexity and Contradiction,* 43. The most significant use of the term "ordinary" occurs in the phrase VSBA coined for its work, "Ugly and Ordinary." See part 2 of *Learning from Las Vegas.*

26. Venturi, Scott Brown, Izenour, *Learning from Las Vegas,* 129.

27. Ibid., 131.

28. Ibid., 93.

29. Ibid., 130.

30. Ibid., 130.

31. Ibid., 74.

32. Ibid., 87.

33. Venturi, "Residence in Chestnut Hill," 30–31.

34. For discussion of such perception, see, for example, Marshall McLuhan and Quentin Fiore, *The Medium Is the Message* (New York: Bantam, 1967), and Marshall McLuhan, *Understanding Media: The Extensions of Man* (New York: Signet Books, 1964).

35. Venturi, *Complexity and Contradiction,* 16. Venturi considered these conditions necessary for a contemporary practice in architecture that was "complex and contradictory in its very inclusion of the traditional Vitruvian elements of commodity, firmness, and delight. And today the wants of program, structure, mechanical equipment, and expression, even in single buildings in simple contexts, are diverse and conflicting in ways previously unimaginable." Ibid.

36. Curtis, *Modern Architecture,* 376.

37. Ibid. The attention VSBA paid to client tastes was fed by a 1960s public dissatisfaction with the modern movement. This dissatisfaction often took the form of complaints against abstraction and the lack of recognizable imagery. Ibid., 377. According to Curtis, *Complexity and Contradiction* was "a handbook of sensibility for a generation bored by the blandness of what they called 'orthodox modern architecture.'" Ibid., 351.

38. Ibid., 376.

39. Ibid.

40. Crosbie, "Shaping Our Thinking—and Buildings," 149.

41. Ibid.

42. Scott Brown, "Preface to the Revised Edition," xvii.

43. See, for example, Haig Beck, "Elitist," *Architectural Design* 11 (1976): 662–66, and David Gebhard, "Venturi Rauch Scott Brown," *Venturi, Rauch and Scott Brown* (Dec. 1981): 205–7.

44. Colquhoun, *Essays in Architectural Criticism,* 140–41.

45. Curtis, *Modern Architecture,* 376.

46. Ibid., 379–80. Curtis indicates a similar concern about other architects' work at the time as well. Ibid., 354.

47. Venturi was criticized for imbuing his architecture with "extensive references to Mannerism, Rococo or Pop Art, which Venturi admitted in *Complexity and Contradiction.*" Von Moos, "A Postscript on History," 204. Scully also described the design process used in the Vanna Venturi House as highly personal. Scully, "Everybody Needs Everything," 53.

48. Colquhoun, "Sign and Substance," 141–42.

49. Gebhard, "Venturi Rauch Scott Brown," 206–7.

50. Ibid.

51. Robert Venturi, *Mother's House,* 35.

52. Von Moos, "A Postscript on History," 202.

53. Colquhoun, *Essays in Architectural Criticism,* 141.

54. Ibid., 150.

55. Ibid., 16–17.

56. Many critics and philosophers have commented on the loss of presence, of the phenomenal, and, generally, of certain dimensions of our bodily experience as a serious concern. See, for example, Jean Baudrillard, *Simulations,* trans. Paul Foss, Paul Patton, and Philip Beitchman (New York: Semiotext(e), 1983).

57. Venturi, *Complexity and Contradiction,* 104.

58. August Heckscher, as quoted in Venturi, *Complexity and Contradiction,* 104.

59. Venturi, *Complexity and Contradiction,* 16.

Conclusion

1. Giedion, *Space, Time, and Architecture,* 428.

2. Ibid., 427.

3. Ibid., 431.

4. Ibid., 432.

5. Bernard Hoesli's comparison of one of Le Corbusier's still lifes with the Villa Stein at Garches demonstrated certain correspondences in the characteristics of space they generated. See Hoesli's analysis in Colin Rowe and Robert Slutzky, *Transparenz,* trans. Bernhard Hoesli (Basil: Birkhauser, 1968), 48–49.

6. See the discussion in Rowe, *Mathematics of the Ideal Villa,* 159–83. See also Anthony Vidler, "Transparency," in *Anyone,* ed. Cynthia C. Davidson (New York: Rizzoli, 1991), 230–39.

7. In *The Hunchback of Notre Dame,* Victor Hugo argued that "This will kill that," meaning that the book would replace architecture's didactic function. It is interesting to note that Wright had a great regard for Hugo.

8. Choay, *Le Corbusier,* 19–21.

9. Besides the viewer's movement, however, architecture shares certain characteristics with machines and other moving objects that make it seem capable of movement. The villas and maisons of the 1920s appear light like an airplane and, at times, project the image of speed, like a fast-moving car. They are airy and seem capable of lifting off in a strong breeze. Architecture becomes buoyant and seems more related to air than to the earth.

10. Sennett, *The Conscience of the Eye,* 103–6.

11. See Gaston Bachelard, *The Poetics of Space,* trans. Maria Jolas (Boston: Beacon Press, 1969).

12. Some of these spaces, such as the stairs in the Vanna Venturi House, have significant consequences for the body as well as for the experience of the imagined body that subjects project.

13. "Preface," Michael Benedikt, ed., *Buildings and Reality: Architecture in the Age of Information,* Center for the Study of American Architecture (Austin, Texas), vol. 4 (New York: Rizzoli, 1988), 6.

14. The body has played an important role in architectural theory from its very beginnings. Religious buildings, for example, are generally designed around a path or

procession to some end goal that is often occupied by an object either accessible or denied; the journey and approach sets up the physical conditions that allude to and support the possibility of transcendence. For example, Terragni's Danteum depends on the subject's walking a path for the successful experience of Terragni's reading of Dante's *Inferno*.

15. Michael Graves, "A Case for Figurative Architecture," in *Michael Graves: Buildings and Projects 1966-1981,* ed. Karen Vogel Wheeler, Peter Arnell, and Ted Bickford (New York: Rizzoli, 1982, 11-13.

16. Anthony Vidler, "The Building in Pain: The Body and Architecture in Post-Modern Culture," *AA Files* 19 (Spring 1990): 3-10.

17. Vidler used a conceptual construction of the body's projection into space and onto objects that was similar to that proposed by Elaine Scarry. See Elaine Scarry, *The Body in Pain: The Making and Unmaking of the World* (New York: Oxford University Press, 1987).

18. Robert McAnulty, "Body Troubles," in *Strategies in Architectural Thinking,* ed. John Whiteman, Jeffrey Kipnis, and Richard Burdett (Cambridge, Mass.: MIT Press, 1992), 180-97; Alberto Perez-Gomez, "The Renovation of the Body: John Hejduk and the Cultural Relevance of Theoretical Projects," *AA Files* 13:26-29.

19. This was a significant concern, for example, for Heidegger; his introduction of the concept of *Dasein* was intended to overcome the problems associated with the split between being and knowing, which were separated in philosophy into the studies of ontology and epistemology, respectively.

20. Vincent Scully, "Note to the Second Edition," in Venturi, *Complexity and Contradiction,* 11-12.

21. Note the separation of hand and eye by new technology in the nineteenth century. This signals a separation between the senses that many people continue to fear and others resist or attempt to repair. This is an issue in VSBA's argument that new technologies, such as the automobile, transformed movement and viewing. The automobile reduced as well as added certain dimensions of experience and, in so doing, transformed the nature of perception.

22. See Russell Sturgis, *Dictionary of Architecture and Building: Biographical, Historical, and Descriptive* (New York: Macmillan, 1901-2).

23. Sennett argued that for Giedion's near contemporary Geoffrey Scott, bodily movement was the secret in defining human scale in the environment, a secret he thought Renaissance architects and theorists understood and modern planners did not. In *The Architecture of Humanism,* Scott wrote, "We project ourselves into [the spaces in which we stand], fill them ideally with our movement." Geoffrey Scott, as quoted in Sennett, *The Conscience of the Eye,* 104.

24. Henri Lefebvre, *The Production of Space,* trans. Donald Nicholson-Smith (Cambridge: Basil Blackwell, 1991), 182–83. These are projective and interpellative experiences. Recently, such authors as Scarry, Lefebvre, Borradori, and Diller and Scofidio have explored some of these ideas.

25. Fisher, "Democratic Social Space," 67. He extends this to the society at large. See 64–65.

26. Louis Althusser, *Lenin and Philosophy and Other Essays* (London: New Left Books, 1971), 174.

27. Horace B. English and Ava Champney English, *Comprehensive Dictionary of Psychological and Psychoanalytical Terms: A Guide to Usage* (New York: David McKay, 1958), 412.

28. J. S. Grotstein, *Splitting and Projective Identification* (New York: Jason Aronson, 1981), 123.

29. Rudolph Arnheim, *Art and Visual Perception: A Psychology of the Creative Eye* (Berkeley: University of California Press, 1974), 448.

30. See Wilhelm Worringer, *Abstraction and Empathy: A Contribution to the Psychology of Style,* trans. Michael Bullock (New York: Meridian Books, 1967).

31. Ruskin, *Seven Lamps,* 43–44.

32. Scarry, *The Body in Pain,* 281 (first quote), 283 (second quote), 285 (third quote).

33. The modes of experience are primarily optical and bodily.

34. Wigley, "The Translation of Architecture," 7.

35. Derrida, in Wigley, "Jacques Derrida: Invitation to a Discussion," 13.

36. Wigley, "The Translation of Architecture," 7.

37. Wigley, "Jacques Derrida: Invitation to a Discussion," 14.

38. Wigley, "The Translation of Architecture," 7.

39. See Clare Cooper Marcus, *House as a Mirror of Self: Exploring the Deeper Meaning of Home* (Berkeley: Conari Press, 1995).

40. Etlin, *Frank Lloyd Wright and Le Corbusier,* 34.

41. Venturi, *Complexity and Contradiction,* 13.

42. See, for example, Peter Eisenman, *House X* (New York: Rizzoli, 1982).

43. Dana Cuff, "Through the Looking Glass," in *Architects' People,* ed. Russell Ellis and Dana Cuff (New York: Oxford University Press, 1989), 69.

44. Hays, *Modernism and the Posthumanist Subject,* 4.

45. Frank Gehry, "Hook, Line, and Signature," in *Anyone,* ed. Cynthia C. Davidson (New York: Rizzoli, 1991), 188. The acceptance of architecture in the twentieth century as an art form often depended on the architect's ability to produce work that was identifiable as his or hers, such as the work we have examined in this book.

46. Ibid.

47. Ibid. Both modernism and postmodernism emerged in the aftermath of a critique of the prescriptions inherited from the past. In the case of modernism, it was classical theory; in the case of postmodernism, it was modernism itself. During both of these periods, architects were forced to redefine their roles and the nature and purpose of architecture itself. A wide array of positions and theories emerged in response to the lack of authority of the traditions being criticized. In the latter part of the twentieth century, architects who no longer adhered to the tenets of modernism had to find new rules. Some turned to the vernacular or commonplace buildings, usually those not designed by trained architects, as the basis for a meaningful architecture. What they considered to be collective or popular culture artifacts, however, were criticized as personal, private, and hermetic works whose meaning was at least partially inaccessible to others.

48. Sennett, *The Conscience of the Eye,* 108–9.

49. Mark Wigley, "Deconstructivist Architecture," in Johnson and Wigley, *Deconstructivist Architecture,* 18.

50. It is not necessary for the study of the imagined subject, however, to put aside that part of architectural design that is autobiographical. To do so would repeat the mistake that Rossi made and would eliminate one of architecture's important, perhaps essential, conditions. The exclusion of personal ideas, values, and associations would not improve our understanding of the imagined subjects that we have gleaned from the various architects' texts; it would eviscerate our understanding and prevent us from benefiting from a more thorough examination of the projections that architects make in their work. The study of the imagined subject would help us examine the possible correlations or lack of them between the projections that architects make and those that subjects, individual or collective, make.

51. Moneo, "Aldo Rossi," 19–20.

52. Ellen Lupton and J. Abbott Miller, "The ABCs of [yellow triangle] [red square] [blue circle]: The Bauhaus and Design Theory," in *The ABCs of [yellow triangle] [red square] [blue circle]: The Bauhaus and Design Theory,* Writing/Culture Monograph 5, ed. Ellen Lupton and J. Abbott Miller (New York: Cooper Union, 1991), 3.

53. Ibid.

54. Kenneth Frampton, *Modern Architecture: A Critical History* (New York: Oxford University Press, 1980), 223.

55. Ibid.

BIBLIOGRAPHY

Agrest, Diana. "Architecture from Without: Body, Logic, and Sex." *Assemblage* 7 (1988): 29–41.

Althusser, Louis. *Lenin and Philosophy and Other Essays.* London: New Left Books, 1971.

Arnell, Peter, and Ted Bickford, eds. *Aldo Rossi: Buildings and Projects.* New York: Rizzoli, 1985.

Arnheim, Rudolf. *Art and Visual Perception: A Psychology of the Creative Eye.* Berkeley: University of California Press, 1974.

Bakhtin, Mikhail Mikhailovich. "Discourse in the Novel." In *Art and Its Significance: An Anthology of Aesthetic Theory,* ed. Stephen David Ross, 484–97. 2d ed. Albany: State University of New York Press, 1987.

Banham, Reyner. *Theory and Design in the First Machine Age.* 2d ed. Cambridge, Mass.: MIT Press, 1983.

Bataille, Georges. *Visions of Excess: Selected Writings 1927–39.* Trans. Allan Stoekl. Minneapolis: University of Minnesota Press, 1985.

Beck, Haig. "Elitist." *Architectural Design* 11 (1976): 662–66.

Benedikt, Michael, ed. *Buildings and Reality: Architecture in the Age of Information.* Center for the Study of American Architecture (Austin, Texas), vol. 4. New York: Rizzoli, 1988.

Borradori, G. "Towards an Architecture of Exile: A Conversation with

Jean-François Lyotard." In *Restructuring Architectural Theory,* ed. M. Diani and C. Ingraham, 12–17. Evanston: Northwestern University Press, 1989.

Bradbury, Ronald. *The Romantic Theories of Architecture of the Nineteenth Century, in Germany, England and France.* New York: AMS Press, 1976.

Buck-Morss, Susan. *The Dialectics of Seeing: Walter Benjamin and the Arcades Project.* Cambridge, Mass.: MIT Press, 1991.

Certeau, Michel de. "Practices of Space." In *On Signs,* ed. Marshall Blonsky, 122–45. Baltimore: Johns Hopkins University Press, 1985.

Choay, Françoise. *Le Corbusier.* New York: Braziller, 1960.

Collins, Peter. *Changing Ideals in Modern Architecture: 1750–1950.* Montreal: McGill-Queen's University Press, 1984.

Colomina, Beatriz. *Privacy and Publicity: Modern Architecture as Mass Media.* Cambridge, Mass.: MIT Press, 1994.

———. "The Split Wall: Domestic Voyeurism." In *Sexuality and Space,* ed. Beatriz Colomina, 72–128. Princeton: Princeton Architectural Press, 1992.

Colquhoun, Alan. *Essays in Architectural Criticism: Modern Architecture and Historical Change.* Cambridge, Mass.: MIT Press, 1981.

———. "Rational Architecture." *Architectural Design* 45, no. 6 (1975): 365–70.

Cooper Marcus, Clare. *House as a Mirror of Self: Exploring the Deeper Meaning of Home.* Berkeley: Conari Press, 1995.

Copjec, Joan. *Read My Desire: Lacan against the Historicists.* Cambridge, Mass.: MIT Press, 1994.

Crosbie, Michael J. "Shaping Our Thinking—and Buildings." *Architecture* (Dec. 1987): 147–49.

Cuff, Dana. "Through the Looking Glass." In *Architects' People,* ed. Russell Ellis and Dana Cuff, 64–102. New York: Oxford University Press, 1989.

Curtis, William J. R. *Modern Architecture since 1900.* 2d ed. Englewood Cliffs, N.J.: Prentice-Hall, 1987.

Dal Co, Francesco. "Criticism and Design." Trans. Diane Ghirardo. *Oppositions* 13 (Summer 1978): 1–16.

Dallmayr, Fred R. *Twilight of Subjectivity: Contributions to a Post-Individualist Theory of Politics.* Amherst: University of Massachusetts Press, 1981.

Derrida, Jacques. "The Double Session." In *A Derrida Reader: Between the Blinds,* ed. Peggy Kamuf, 171–99. New York: Columbia University Press, 1991.

———. *Of Grammatology.* Trans. Gayatri Chakravorty Spivak. Baltimore: Johns Hopkins University Press, 1976.

———. "Point de Folie—Maintenant l'architecture." *AA Files* 12 (1986): 65–75.

Diani, Marco, and Catherine Ingraham. "Introduction: Edifying Projects: Restructuring Architectural Theory." In *Restructuring Architectural Theory,* ed. Marco Diani and Catherine Ingraham, 1–6. Evanston: Northwestern University Press, 1989.

Dunster, David, ed. *Venturi and Rauch.* Architectural Monographs 1. London: Academy Editions, 1978.

Eisenman, Peter. "Editor's Introduction: The Houses of Memory, The Texts of Analogy." In Aldo Rossi, *The Architecture of the City,* trans. Diane Ghirardo, 2–11. Cambridge, Mass.: MIT Press, 1991.

———. "En Terror Firma: In Trails of Grotextes." *The Fifth Column 7* 1 (Oct. 1988): 24–27.

———. *House X.* New York: Rizzoli, 1982.

Ellis, Russell, and Dana Cuff, eds. *Architects' People.* New York: Oxford University Press, 1989.

English, Horace B., and Ava Champney English. *Comprehensive Dictionary of Psychological and Psychoanalytical Terms: A Guide to Usage.* New York: David McKay, 1958.

Etlin, Richard. *Frank Lloyd Wright and Le Corbusier: The Romantic Legacy.* New York: Manchester University Press, 1994.

Filler, Martin. "Rossi Secco and Rossi Dolce." *Art in America* (March 1980): 100-106.

Fisher, Philip. "Democratic Social Space: Whitman, Melville, and the Promise of American Transparency." *Representations* 24 (Fall 1988): 64-76.

Forster, Kurt W. "Antiquity and Modernity in the La Roche-Jeanneret Houses of 1923." *Oppositions* 15/16 (Winter/Spring 1979): 131-53.

Foster, Hal, ed. *Vision and Visuality.* Seattle: Bay Press, 1988.

Foucault, Michel. "Of Other Spaces." *Diacritic* 16, no. 1 (Spring 1986): 22-27.

Frampton, Kenneth. "Editor's Introduction." *Oppositions* 15/16 (Winter/Spring 1979): 5-7.

———. *Modern Architecture: A Critical History.* New York: Oxford University Press, 1980.

Frampton, Kenneth, ed. *Aldo Rossi in America: 1976-1979.* Institute for Architecture and Urban Studies Catalogue 2. New York: Institute for Architecture and Urban Studies, 1979.

Futagawa, Yukio. *Venturi and Rauch.* Global Architecture 39. Tokyo: A.D.A. Edita, 1976.

Gasché, Rodolphe. *The Tain of the Mirror: Derrida and the Philosophy of Reflection.* Cambridge, Mass.: Harvard University Press, 1986.

Gebhard, David. "Venturi Rauch Scott Brown." *Venturi, Rauch and Scott Brown* (Dec. 1981): 205-7.

Gehry, Frank. "Hook, Line, and Signature." In *Anyone,* ed. Cynthia C. Davidson, 186-95. New York: Rizzoli, 1991.

Ghirardo, Diane. "Introduction: The Theater of Shadows." In *Aldo Rossi: 1981-1991,* ed. Morris Adjmi, 11-15. New York: Princeton Architectural Press, 1991.

Giedion, Sigfried. *Mechanization Takes Command.* New York: Norton, 1984.

———. *Space, Time and Architecture: The Growth of a New Tradition.* 4th ed. Cambridge, Mass.: Harvard University Press, 1963.

Gifford, Don, ed. *The Literature of Architecture: The Evolution of Architectural Theory and Practice in Nineteenth-Century America.* New York: Dutton, 1966.

Graves, Michael. "A Case for Figurative Architecture." In *Michael Graves: Buildings and Projects 1966-1981,* ed. Karen Vogel Wheeler, Peter Arnell, and Ted Bickford, 11-13. New York: Rizzoli, 1982.

Grotstein, J. S. *Splitting and Projective Identification.* New York: Jason Aronson, 1981.

Hays, K. Michael. *Modernism and the Posthumanist Subject: The Architecture of Hannes Meyer and Ludwig Hilberseimer.* Cambridge, Mass.: MIT Press, 1992.

Henderson, Philip. *William Morris: His Life, Work, and Friends.* London: Thames and Hudson, 1967.

Hildebrand, Grant. *Origins of Architectural Pleasure.* Berkeley: University of California Press, 1999.

———. *The Wright Space: Pattern and Meaning in Frank Lloyd Wright's Houses.* Seattle: University of Washington Press, 1991.

Hollier, Denis. *Against Architecture: The Writings of Georges Bataille.* Trans. Betsy Wing. Cambridge, Mass.: MIT Press, 1989.

Jencks, Charles. *Le Corbusier and the Tragic View of Architecture.* Cambridge, Mass.: Harvard University Press, 1974.

Johnson, Philip, and Mark Wigley. *Deconstructivist Architecture.* New York: Museum of Modern Art, 1988.

Kaufmann, Edgar, and Ben Raeburn, eds. *Frank Lloyd Wright: Writings and Buildings.* New York: New American Library, 1974.

Kerby, Anthony Paul. *Narrative and the Self.* Bloomington: Indiana University Press, 1991.

Knesl, John. "Postclassical *Poesis.*" *Pratt Journal of Architecture* 2 (Spring 1988): 163-75.

Krauss, Rosalind. "The Im/Pulse to See." In *Vision and Visuality,* ed. Hal Foster, 51-78. Seattle: Bay Press, 1988.

Kuspit, Donald B. "The Unhappy Consciousness of Modernism." *Artforum* (Jan. 1981): 53-37.

Lacan, Jacques. *Écrits: A Selection.* Trans. Alan Sheridan. New York: Norton, 1977.
———. *The Four Fundamental Concepts of Psycho-Analysis.* Ed. Jacques-Alain Miller. Trans. Alan Sheridan. New York: Norton, 1981.
La Marche, Jean. *The Desire of Our Eyes.* Berkeley: Person-Environment Theory Series, Center for Environmental Design Research, 1992.
———. "In and Out of Type." In *Ordering Space: Types in Architecture and Design,* ed. Karen Franck and Lynda Schneekloth, 209–31. New York: Van Nostrand Reinhold, 1994.
———. *Self and Surface: The Mirror of Architecture.* Berkeley: Person-Environment Theory Series, Center for Environmental Design Research, 1993.
Le Corbusier. *Modulor I and II.* Trans. Peter De Francia and Anna Bostock. Cambridge, Mass.: Harvard University Press, 1980.
———. *Towards a New Architecture.* Trans. Frederick Etchells. New York: Dover, 1986.
———. "Towards a New Architecture: Guiding Principles (1920)." In *Programs and Manifestoes on Twentieth-Century Architecture,* ed. Ulrich Conrads. Cambridge, Mass.: MIT Press, 1993.
———. *Vers une architecture.* Rev. ed. Paris: G. Crès, 1924.
Lefebvre, Henri. *The Production of Space.* Trans. Donald Nicholson-Smith. Cambridge: Basil Blackwell, 1991.
Levinas, E. *The Levinas Reader.* Ed. Sean Hand. Cambridge, Mass.: Basil Blackwell, 1989.
Loos, Adolf. "Ornament and Crime." In Ludwig Münz and Gustav Künstler, *Adolf Loos: Pioneer of Modern Architecture,* 226–31. New York: Praeger, 1966.
Lupton, Ellen, and J. Abbott Miller, eds. *The ABCs of [yellow triangle] [red square] [blue circle]: The Bauhaus and Design Theory.* Writing/Culture Monograph 5. New York: Cooper Union, 1991.
Lyotard, Jean-François. *The Inhuman: Reflections on Time.* Trans. Geoffrey Bennington and Rachel Bowlby. Stanford: Stanford University Press, 1991.
McAnulty, Robert. "Body Troubles." In *Strategies in Architectural Thinking,* ed. John Whiteman, Jeffrey Kipnis, and Richard Burdett, 180–97. Cambridge, Mass.: MIT Press, 1992.
Mitchell, Juliet, and Jacqueline Rose, eds. *Jacques Lacan, Feminine Sexuality.* New York: Norton, 1985.
Moneo, Rafael. "Aldo Rossi: The Idea of Architecture and the Modena Cemetery." Trans. Angela Giral. *Oppositions* (Summer 1976): 1–30.
Moos, Stanislaus von. "A Postscript on History, 'Architecture Parlante' and Populism." *Venturi, Rauch and Scott Brown* (Dec. 1981): 199–204.
Morton, David. "Tendenza." *Progressive Architecture* (Oct. 1980): 49–62.
Mulvey, Laura. "Topographies of the Mask and Curiosity." In *Sexuality and Space,* ed. Beatriz Colomina, 52–71. Princeton: Princeton Architectural Press, 1992.
Norberg-Schulz, Christian. *Meaning in Western Architecture.* New York: Rizzoli, 1983.
O'Donnell, Sheila. "Introduction." In *Aldo Rossi: Selected Writings and Projects,* ed. John O'Regan, Paul Keogh, Sheila O'Donnell, and Shane O'Toole. Dublin: Gandon Editions, 1983.
Papadakis, Andreas, Catherine Cooke, and Andrew Benjamin, eds. *Deconstruction: Omnibus Volume.* New York: Rizzoli, 1989.
Perez-Gomez, Alberto. "The Renovation of the Body: John Hejduk and the Cultural Relevance of Theoretical Projects." *AA Files* 13:26–29.
Pfeiffer, Bruce Brooks, ed. *Frank Lloyd Wright Collected Writings.* 5 vols. New York: Rizzoli, 1992.
Placzek, Adolf K., ed. *Macmillan Encyclopedia of Architects.* 4 vols. New York: Free Press, 1982.
Quinan, Jack. "Frank Lloyd Wright, Darwin D. Martin, and the Creation of the Martin House." *Prairie House Journal* (April 1987): 5–12.
Rossi, Aldo. "An Analogical Architecture." *Architecture and Urbanism* 56 (May 1976): 74.

———. *The Architecture of the City.* Trans. Diane Ghirardo. Cambridge, Mass.: MIT Press, 1991.

———. "The Blue of the Sky." Trans. Marlene Barsoum and Liviu Dimitriu. *Oppositions* (Summer 1976): 31–34.

———. *A Scientific Autobiography.* Trans. Lawrence Venuti. Cambridge, Mass.: MIT Press, 1981.

———. "Thoughts about My Recent Work." *Architecture and Urbanism* 56 (May 1976): 83.

Rowe, Colin. *The Mathematics of the Ideal Villa and Other Essays.* Cambridge, Mass.: MIT Press, 1985.

———. "Robert Venturi and the Yale Mathematics Building." *Oppositions* (Fall 1976): 1–23.

Rowe, Colin, and Fred Koetter. "Collage City." *Architectural Review* 158, no. 942 (August 1975): 66–90.

Rowe, Colin, and Robert Slutzky. *Transparenz.* Trans. Bernhard Hoesli. Basil: Birkhauser, 1968.

Ruskin, John. *The Seven Lamps of Architecture.* New York: Farrar, Straus and Giroux, 1974.

Sarbib, Jean Louis. "Popu-lore architecture." *L'Architecture d'aujourd'hui* (June 1978): 2–6.

———. "Venturi and Rauch as Planners: An Analysis of a Few Recent P[l]anning Projects." *L'Architecture d'aujourd'hui* (June 1978): 76–79.

Scarry, Elaine. *The Body in Pain: The Making and Unmaking of the World.* New York: Oxford University Press, 1987.

Schwartz, Frederic, ed. *Mother's House: The Evolution of Vanna Venturi's House in Chestnut Hill.* New York: Rizzoli, 1992.

Scott Brown, Denise. "On Architectural Formalism and Social Concern: A Discourse for Social Planners and Radical Chic Architects." *Oppositions* (Summer 1976): 99–112.

Scully, Vincent. "Everybody Needs Everything." In *Mother's House: The Evolution of Vanna Venturi's House in Chestnut Hill,* ed. Frederic Schwartz, 39–57. New York: Rizzoli, 1992.

———. "Introduction" and "Note to the Second Edition." In Robert Venturi, *Complexity and Contradiction in Architecture,* 9–12. 2d ed. New York: Museum of Modern Art, 1979.

———. "Postscript: Ideology in Form." In Aldo Rossi, *A Scientific Autobiography,* trans. Lawrence Venuti, 111–16. Cambridge, Mass.: MIT Press, 1981.

Sennett, Richard. *The Conscience of the Eye.* New York: Norton, 1992.

———. *Flesh and Stone: The Body and the City in Western Civilization.* New York: Norton, 1994.

Shane, Grahame. "Contextualism." *Architectural Design* 11 (1976): 676–79.

Sullivan, Louis. *Kindergarten Chats and Other Writings.* New York: Dover, 1979.

Taylor, Mark C. "The Subject of Architecture." In *Anyone,* ed. Cynthia C. Davidson, 136–45. New York: Rizzoli, 1991.

Thoreau, Henry David. *Walden.* New York: Macmillan, 1962.

Trilling, Lionel. *The Experience of Literature: A Reader with Commentaries.* New York: Doubleday, 1967.

Tschumi, Bernard. *Architecture and Disjunction.* Cambridge, Mass.: MIT Press, 1991.

Venturi, Robert. "Architecture as Shelter, Decoration on It, and Another Plea for a Symbolism of the Ordinary in Architecture." *L'Architecture d'aujourd'hui* (June 1978): 12–19.

———. *Complexity and Contradiction in Architecture.* 2d ed. New York: Museum of Modern Art, 1979.

———. "Learning the Right Lessons from the Beaux-Arts." *Architectural Design* 1 (1979): 25.

———. "Residence in Chestnut Hill." In *Mother's House: The Evolution of Vanna Venturi's House in Chestnut Hill,* ed. Frederic Schwartz, 30–33. New York: Rizzoli, 1992.

Venturi, Robert, and Denise Scott Brown. *A View from the Campidoglio: Selected Essays, 1953–1984.* New York: Harper and Row, 1984.

Venturi, Robert, Denise Scott Brown, and Steven Izenour. *Learning from Las Vegas: The Forgotten Symbolism of Architectural Form.* Rev. ed. Cambridge, Mass.: MIT Press, 1985.

Vidler, Anthony. *The Architectural Uncanny: Essays in the Modern Unhomely.* Cambridge, Mass.: MIT Press, 1994.

———. "The Building in Pain: The Body and Architecture in Post-Modern Culture." *AA Files* 19 (Spring 1990): 3–10.

———. "Transparency." In *Anyone,* ed. Cynthia C. Davidson, 230–39. New York: Rizzoli, 1991.

Wigley, Mark. "Jacques Derrida: Invitation to a Discussion." *Columbia Documents of Architecture and Theory: D* 1 (1992): 7–22.

———. "The Translation of Architecture: The Product of Babel." *Architectural Design* 60, nos. 9–10 (1990): 6–13.

———. "Untitled: The Housing of Gender." In *Sexuality and Space,* ed. Beatriz Colomina, 327–89. Princeton: Princeton Architectural Press, 1992.

Worringer, Wilhelm. *Abstraction and Empathy: A Contribution to the Psychology of Style.* Trans. Michael Bullock. New York: Meridian Books, 1967.

Zizek, Slavoj. *Looking Awry: An Introduction to Jacques Lacan through Popular Culture.* Cambridge, Mass.: MIT Press, 1992.

INDEX

Acropolis (Athens), 52, *53*, 110
aesthetics: correlated with the body, 106;
  projection in early twentieth-century theories, 107–8. *See also* visual (aesthetic) preferences
Affleck House (Wright), 123n.43
Albers, Josef, 128n.4
Allen Memorial Art Museum addition
  (VSBA), 7
Althusser, Louis, 107
Anguish of Departure, The (de Chirico), *73*
Appleton, Jay, 123n.39
Arab architecture, 44
*Architectural Uncanny, The: Essays in the Mod-
  ern Unhomely* (Vidler), 5
architecture: Arab, 44; associations in, 90;
  autobiography in, 110–14, 132n.50; body
  terms in, 105–6; buildings portraying their
  clients, 21–23; classical, 8, 102; as collective
  artifact, 9; in construction of the subject
  for Derrida, 10, 108, 109, 115; defamiliariz-
  ing, 4, 5, 7; equilibrium of diverse interests
  in, 81, 82; for expressing the new, 100;
  Gothic, 102, 122n.9; honesty in, 8; imagin-
  ing subject of, 115–16, 132n.50; Leonardo
  da Vinci's "Vitruvian man" and experience of, 1–2; mathematics as basis of Le
  Corbusier's, 41, 124n.23; meaning in, 114–
  15; as multifunctioning, 9; multiple interests in, 8–9; multiple voices embodied in,
  9; organic, 13, 14, 16, 122n.9; philosophy
  using metaphors from, 108–9; presence in,
  27, 35, 104–5, 109; presence of absence in,
  74; signature work, 110, 111–12, 132n.45;
  Soviet, 63; traversing, 103, 130n.9; Tschumi on movement in experience of, 3–5;
  unavoidability of, 109. *See also* modernist
  architecture; postmodern architecture;
  and architects by name

construction of the subject, 10, 108, 109, 115; on barbarity, 5–6; on meaning as undecidable, 114; on questioning the familiar, 6
difficult wholes, 81, 87, 98
Duchamp, Marcel, 118n.29
duck, the, 92, *93*

École des Beaux-Arts, 124n.29
"economy of means," 5, 41, 125n.36
Eisenman, Peter, 64, 75–76, 108, 110–11
Elementary School at Fagnano Olona, Italy (Rossi): the body in plan of, 104; courtyard, *67;* plan, *67;* reductiveness of, 64; stairs in courtyard, *68;* view from interior, *68*
Eliot, T. S., 81
Ellis, Russell, 22
Emerson, Ralph Waldo, 14
empathy, 107–8
Empress of France (ship), *54*
Etchells, Frederick, 38
Etlin, Richard, 26–27, 48–49, 110, 125nn. 35, 44
exterior and interior. *See* interior and exterior

Fagnano Olona, Italy, Elementary School (Rossi). *See* Elementary School at Fagnano Olona, Italy
familiar, the: architects turning to in 1970s, 6; artistic exploration of, 118n.29; associations provoked by, 90; cultural variation in, 9; Derrida on questioning, 6; Freud on, 8; Le Corbusier on, 37–38; in Le Corbusier's work, 100; as problematic concept, 8; Rossi in return to, 6–7; in Rossi's work, 57–59, 74, 77–78, 100; in unfamiliar contexts for Venturi, 79, 90; VSBA in return to, 6–7; in VSBA's Guild House, 90; VSBA using as background for the new, 88, 90–91, 94, 100; Wright on, 13–14; in Wright's houses, 36, 100
Farman Goliath airplane, 46, *46*
feminism, 119n.33
Filler, Martin, 127n.21
Fisher, Philip, 16–17, 106, 122n.13
Florence, Roman amphitheater in, 59, *60*
"form follows function," 18, 102, 122n.9
Forster, Kurt, 125n.45
Frampton, Kenneth, 55, 114–15, 126n.59
Freud, Sigmund, 8, 16, 105

Gallaratese 2 (Rossi): de Chirico painting compared with, 127n.21; exterior, *69;* open-air corridor of, 64, 69; plan and elevation drawings, *69;* view down portico, *70*
Gans, Herbert, 80, 118n.27

Gehry, Frank, 104, 111
geometry: in Rossi's work, 64, 69; as universal for Le Corbusier, 49, 52; and VSBA's residual space, 83
gestalt psychology, 7, 76, 81, 92
Giedion, Sigfried: on architecture reuniting thinking and feeling, 2–3, 39, 101, 126n.8; on bird's-eye view, 101; on dynamics as essence of new age, 103; on space-time, 124n.25; Tschumi compared with, 4; on value of architecture, 8; on world mirroring our inner states, 106
Gifford, Don, 14, 122n.9
glass, 15, 22, 112
Gothic architecture, 102, 122n.9
Gropius, Walter, 103
Guild House (Venturi and Rauch, Cope and Lippincott, Associated Architects): accommodations in, 85, 87; communication through conventions in, 94; as decorated shed, 92; entrance, *89;* entrance detail, *89;* exterior, *88;* the familiar in, 90; first-floor plan, *88;* habitual perception of distance disturbed in, 90; ornament in, 90; TV antenna of, 96, *97;* windows of, 90

Halbwachs, Maurice, 76
Hays, K. Michael, 3, 111, 126n.8
Heidegger, Martin, 6, 108, 131n.19
Henderson, Philip, 122n.9
Heurtley, Arthur, House (Wright): diagrammatic drawing of movement in, *33;* exterior, *32;* path from exterior to hearth, 27; plan, *32*
Hickox, Warren, House (Wright), *29*
Hildebrand, Grant, 123n.39
Himmelblau, Coop, 104
Hoesli, Bernard, 130n.5
Hopper, Edward, *113*
Hugo, Victor, 130n.7
human body. *See* body, the

interior and exterior: modernist architecture disrupting, 112–13; Sullivan on, 18; Venturi on poché and, 82–83; Wright on, 15, 16–17, 18–21, 26
interpellation, 106–7, 113, 115
"In the Cause of Architecture" (Wright): on buildings portraying the clients, 22; as early work, 99; as introduction to architectural thinking, 11; republication of, 120n.41; significance of, 120n.40
iron, 15, 108
Izenour, Steven, 119n.38

Japanese Print, The (Wright), 120n.41
Jeffersonian democracy, 122n.13, 123n.26
Jencks, Charles, 55, 56
Johnson, Philip C., 121n.44

Kahn, Louis: on poché, 82, 83, 128n.13; Salk Institute Community Center, 82, *82, 83;* on silence, 74

Kaufmann, Edgar, Jr., 120n.41

Kindergarten Chats (Sullivan), 18

Larkin Company Administration Building (Wright), *20, 22*

Learning from Las Vegas (Venturi, Scott Brown, and Izenour): coauthors for, 80; and *Complexity and Contradiction in Architecture,* 128n.7; on difficult wholes, 81–82; Scott Brown's contributions to, 119n.38; significance of, 120n.40, 121n.44; on symbolism in architecture, 94, 96; visual emphasis of, 92

Le Corbusier, 37–56; assumed names of, 55; autobiography in work of, 110; classical leanings of, 42, 45, 125n.36; clients of, 126n.49; contradictions in, 55–56; on decoration, 40; defamiliarization practiced by, 6; "desire of our eyes," 41, 54, 101; dialectical architecture of, 39, 44–45, 125nn. 35, 36; on École des Beaux-Arts, 125n.29; on the familiar, 37–38; the familiar in work of, 100; on geometry as universal, 49, 52; on harmony between body and mind, 52, 54; human being in work of, 41–43, 125n.36; intellectual and sensorial satisfactions distinguished by, 40, 55; interpellation and work of, 106; Maison Cook, 46, *46;* masculine pronoun used by, 124n.1; on mathematical correspondence between body and universe, 52, 54; on mathematics as basis of architecture, 41, 124n.23; mechanical forms in work of, 45–46, 125n.35; on the modern subject, 39–40; the Modulor, 42, *42, 43;* on new forms, 38, 39; on presence in architecture, 104–5; as producing significant buildings and writings, 10; promenade in work of, 43–44, 46, 48–49, 124n.25, 125nn. 36, 44; Purism, 101, 127n.17; signature work produced by, 112; simultaneity in work of, 101–2; on social revolution, 39; tensions of modern era revealed in, 54–55; on traversing architecture, 103; two human bodies conceptualized by, 42–43; and the unfamiliar, 38, 54–55, 100; universal subject intended by, 55; VSBA compared with, 88, 90; on workplace versus domestic environment, 38–39; Wright on, 36. *See also* Maison La Roche; *Towards a New Architecture;* Villa Savoye; Villa Stein

Ledoux, Claude-Nicolas, 102

Lefebvre, Henri, 105–6

Leonardo da Vinci, 1–2, *2,* 42, 104, 124n.28

Lipp, Theodor, 107–8

Loos, Adolf, 124n.15

Lucca, Roman amphitheater in, 59, *61*

Lupton, Ellen, 114

machines: Le Corbusier on new, 38; mechanical forms in Le Corbusier's work, 45–46, 125n.35; Wright on influence of new, 13, 14–15, 25–26, 121n.1

Maison Cook (Le Corbusier), 46, *46*

Maison La Roche (Le Corbusier): exterior, *48;* interior, *50;* promenade in, 125n.45; topographic experiences in, 48

marché, 124n.29

Marcus, Clare Cooper, 109

Martin, Darwin, 23

Martin, Darwin, House (Wright): as expressive of the client, 22–23; exterior, *23;* plan of complex, 23, *24;* separation of interior spaces in, 27

masonry, 15, 108

materials. *See* construction materials

mathematics: as basis of Le Corbusier's architecture, 41, 124n.23; Le Corbusier on correspondence between body and universe, 52, 54. *See also* geometry

McAnulty, Robert, 104

metaphysics, 109

Meyer, Adolf, 103

Mies van der Rohe, Ludwig, 103

Miller, J. Abbott, 114

modernist architecture: alienation evoked by, 6, 77, 100, 102, 112–13; arising from critique of past, 132n.47; Bauhaus, 114; defamiliarization in, 5, 8; "form follows function," 18, 102, 122n.9; Giedion as voice of, 2–3; interior/exterior distinction disrupted in, 112–13; liberation as intention of, 8, 16, 112; loss of continuity with the past, 7; movement as central concern of, 103; the new as unfamiliar in, 91; public dissatisfaction with, 129n.37; Rossi on, 63; self-expression proscribed in, 110, 111; signs eliminated in, 92; Venturi's *Complexity and Contradiction in Architecture* and decline of, 121n.44; VSBA on the wall in, 128n.13

Modulor, The, 42, *42, 43*

Moneo, Rafael, 70, 114

Monument to the Partisans of World War II (Rossi): perspective, *65;* photograph, *65;* plan, *64;* section, *65;* seen as Purist, 64

Morris, William, 122n.9

Mosque of Bursa, 126n.8

movement: as modernist concern, 103; promenade in Le Corbusier's work, 43–44, 46, 48–49, 124nn. 25, 29, 125nn. 36, 44; technology extending, 100–101, 131n.21; Tschumi on, 3–5; in Wright's houses, 26–27

National Football Hall of Fame project
(VSBA): as decorated shed, 92; model, *94;*
typical elements in, 91, 103
New York Five, 112
Nietzsche, Friedrich, 6, 126n.7
Nîmes, Roman amphitheater in, 59, *60*
Norberg-Schulz, Christian, 26

O'Donnell, Sheila, 127n.21
organic architecture, 13, 14, 16, 122n.9
ornament. *See* decoration
outside and inside. *See* interior and exterior

Parthenon, 40, *40,* 46, *47,* 52, *53*
Pavilion at Borgo Ticino, Italy (Rossi): contextualism of, 69–70; exterior, *71;* plan, *71*
Perez-Gomez, Alberto, 104
philosophy, architectural metaphors in,
108–9
poché, 82–83, 87, 88, 103, 128nn. 9, 11, 13
Pop Art, 90, 91
postmodern architecture: arising from critique of past, 114, 132n.47; deconstructivist architecture, 5, 104; Venturi's writings
and, 121nn. 43, 44
projection, 107–8, 112, 113, 115
promenade, 43–44, 46, 48–49, 124nn. 25, 29,
125nn. 36, 44
prospect-and-refuge theory, 123n.39
psychoanalysis, 107
Purism, 64, 101, 127n.17

queer theory, 119n.33
Quinan, Jack, 22–23

Rasmussen, Steen Eiler, 44
Rauch, John, 119n.38
reader-response theory, 119n.33
reinforced concrete, 15
residual space, 83
Robie, Frederick C., House (Wright): exteri-
or, *34;* interior, *34;* path from exterior to
hearth, 27; plan, *34;* separation of interior
spaces in, 27
Roman amphitheaters: Arles, *59;* Colosseum
in Rome, *62;* Florence, 59, *60;* Lucca, 59,
61; Nîmes, 59, *60;* Rossi on transformation
of, 59
Rome, Colosseum in, *62*
Room in New York (Hopper), *113*
Rossi, Aldo, 57–78; analogical process of, 58,
64; on architecture as repository of human
labor, 8; austerity of work of, 74; autobiography in work of, 59, 61–62, 77; binaries in
work of, 75–76; bourgeois childhood of,
62, 126n.9; cabins at Elba, 63, *63,* 64; on
change, 76; on collective dimensions of
subjectivity, 63, 76–77; contextualism of, 6,

7, 69; on dialectic between people and environment, 76–77; dialectics in work of, 74,
127n.25; erasures in work of, 72, 74, 105;
the familiar in work of, 57–59, 74, 77–78,
100; gestalt figure-ground relationship
used by, 7, 76; as inaccessible, 64; the irrational as interest of, 74–75, 77; Le Corbusier's work contrasted with, 56; on loss of
identity, 61, 126n.8; on modernist architecture, 63; and Nietzsche, 126n.7; as producing significant buildings and writings,
10; Purism associated with, 64, 127n.17;
reductiveness of work of, 64; in return to
the familiar, 6–7; on Roman amphitheaters, 59; *A Scientific Autobiography,* 57, 58,
74–75, 120n.40, 121n.43, 126n.9; scientific
objectivity as aim of, 62–63, 75, 110,
132n.50; signature work produced by, 111,
112; on subjects and objects, 61, 75; on
timeless architecture, 62, 64, 77–78,
126n.7; on typologies, 6, 57–59, 62, 75; the
unfamiliar in work of, 100; VSBA compared with, 88, 90. See also *Architecture of
the City;* Cemetery of San Cataldo; De Amicis School; Elementary School at Fagnano
Olona; Gallaratese 2; Monument to the
Partisans of World War II; Pavilion at Borgo Ticino
Rowe, Colin, 48, 49, 110, 125n.36, 129n.16
Ruskin, John, 8, 15–16, 108

Salk Institute Community Center (Kahn),
82, *82, 83*
Sarbib, Jean Louis, 118n.27
Sargent, John Singer, 22
Scarry, Elaine, 108, 131n.17
Scientific Autobiography, A (Rossi), 57, 58, 74–
75, 120n.40, 121n.43, 126n.9
Scott, Geoffrey, 131n.23
Scott Brown, Denise: multivocal nature of
work of, 80; "Sexism and the Star System
in Architecture," 119n.38; on symbolism in
architecture, 94, 96; in Venturi Scott
Brown and Associates, 10, 119n.38, 128n.3.
See also *Learning from Las Vegas;* Venturi
Scott Brown and Associates
Scully, Vincent, 72, 74–75, 85, 105, 121n.44,
128n.9
semiotics, 102
Sennett, Richard, 9, 103, 112, 119n.34,
131n.23
"Sexism and the Star System in Architecture" (Scott Brown), 119n.38
Shane, Grahame, 129n.16
Short, William, 119n.38
signature work, 110, 111–12, 132n.45
signs: interpretation of, 114; late twentieth-
century interest in, 102; long-standing ar-

82–83, 87, 88, 103, 128nn. 11, 13; populist architecture advocated by, 94, 96; as producing significant buildings and writings, 10; on residual space, 83; in return to the familiar, 6–7; scale and context manipulated by, 91; separation between sign and substance in work of, 97–98, 114; signature work produced by, 112; on signs in architecture, 91, 92, 94, 97–98, 105, 114; on typologies, 88, 90–91, 103; the unfamiliar in work of, 100; on valid architecture, 97; visual focus in work of, 91–92; on whole as array of binaries, 81. *See also* BASCO Showroom; Guild House; National Football Hall of Fame project; Venturi, Vanna, House

Vidler, Anthony, 5, 104, 131n.17

Villa Savoye (Le Corbusier): exterior, *49;* mechanical forms in roof of, 46; promenade, 44, 48, *49, 50,* 125n.45; Venturi's Vanna Venturi House compared with, 128n.14

Villa Stein (Le Corbusier): exterior, *51;* interior, *51;* Le Corbusier still life compared with, 130n.5; mechanical forms in roof of, 46, *47;* spatial rhythms superimposed on plan of, *45;* topographic experiences in, 48

vision: eye and body, 105; projection and interpellation depending on, 108; reduction to the optical, 104; technology extending, 100–101, 131n.21; twentieth-century artistic interest in, 101–2; VSBA's visual focus, 91–92. *See also* visual (aesthetic) preferences

visual (aesthetic) preferences: classical, 106; Le Corbusier on, 38, 41, 43, 54, 55, 101; Wright on architecture and, 14, 15

"Vitruvian man" (Leonardo da Vinci), 1–2, *2,* 42, 104, 124n.28

VSBA. *See* Venturi Scott Brown and Associates

walls, 15, 26, 44, 112, 113, 128n.13

Wasmuth portfolio (Wright), 27, 120n.41

Werkbund Administration Building, 103, 106

Whitman, Walt, 17, 106

Wigley, Mark, 6, 108, 109, 113

Winslow, W. H., House (Wright): exterior, *28;* interior, *29;* path from exterior to hearth, 27; plan, *28*

Wordsworth, William, 90

"Work of Art in the Age of Mechanical Reproduction, The" (Benjamin), 4

Worringer, Wilhelm, 108

Wright, Frank Lloyd, 13–36; Affleck House, 123n.43; "The Art and Craft of the Machine," 11, 120nn. 40, 41; autobiography in work of, 110; Bradley House, *30;* on buildings portraying their clients, 21–23, 35, 123n.27; defamiliarization practiced by, 6; on democracy and architecture, 21, 23, 25, 35; Emerson influencing, 14; on the familiar, 13–14; the familiar in work of, 36, 100; "form follows function," 18, 122n.9; freedom in architecture of, 23, 25–27; Hickox House, *29;* on Hugo, 130n.7; on individuality, 18, 35; on interior and exterior, 15, 16–17, 18–21, 26; *The Japanese Print,* 120n.41; Larkin Company Administration Building, *20,* 22; on Le Corbusier, 36; on materials, 13, 15–16, 26; moral dimension of work of, 102; movement in houses of, 26–27; on organic architecture, 13, 14, 16, 122n.9; on presence of buildings, 27, 35, 104–5; as producing significant buildings and writings, 10; on scale of buildings, 27, 35; separation of interior spaces in houses of, 27; signature work produced by, 112; on traversing architecture, 103; and the unfamiliar, 13, 100; Venturi's Vanna Venturi House compared with Oak Park home of, 128n.14; Wasmuth portfolio, 27, 120n.41. *See also* Barton, George, House; Coonley, Avery, House; Heurtley, Arthur, House; "In the Cause of Architecture"; Martin, Darwin, House; Robie, Frederick C., House; "Sovereignty of the Individual, The"; Thomas, Frank, House; Unity Temple; Winslow, W. H., House

JEAN LA MARCHE teaches architecture and theory at the State University of New York at Buffalo. He has lectured widely on various aspects of modern architecture and has practiced architecture for over thirty years.

The University of Illinois Press
is a founding member of the
Association of American University
Presses.

Composed in 9/14 Stone Serif
with Stone Sans display
at the University of Illinois Press
Designed by Paula Newcomb
Manufactured by
Thomson-Shore, Inc.

University of Illinois Press
1325 South Oak Street
Champaign, IL 61820-6903
www.press.uillinois.edu